A
Woman's
Place

A Woman's Place

An illustrated history of women
at home from the Roman villa to
the Victorian town house

by

MARJORIE FILBEE

EBURY PRESS

London

First published 1980
by Ebury Press
National Magazine House
72 Broadwick Street
London W1V 2BP

ISBN 0 85223 154 7

Drawings by Patrick Filbee
Designed by Derek Morrison
Edited by Isabel Sutherland
Picture research by Beatrice Phillpotts

Cover picture: McIan, *Highland Home Interior in Perthshire,*
courtesy National Museum of Antiquities, Scotland.

Filmset and printed in Great Britain by
BAS Printers Limited, Over Wallop, Hampshire
and bound by
Cambridge University Press, Cambridge.

643

Contents

Key to Illustrations

The figures in brackets within the text refer firstly to the page on which an illustration appears and secondly, where there is more than one illustration on that page, to its position – eg. (99.1) indicates the first illustration on page 99.

The text referring to the illustrations is on the same or facing page in most cases but where it is not, the page where it is to be found is indicated at the end of the caption.

Acknowledgements

My grateful thanks for their help goes to Sally Holden of the North Cornwall Museum, to the curators and staff of the Museum of London, the Welsh Folk Museum, Reading Museum, The Museum of English Rural Life, the Country Life section of the National Museum of Antiquities of Scotland, the Welsh Folk Museum and the National Trust offices for Devon and Cornwall, North Wales and Scotland. My thanks too to the Shakespeare Birthplace Trust for permission to publish the photograph of the dairy at Mary Arden's House; to the Trustees of the late Lord Berkeley for permission to use the photographs of Berkeley Castle; to the Science Museum for permission to use the photograph of an early vacuum cleaner; also to the Dorset Natural History and Archaeological Society for permission to quote from J. S. Cox's books of Dorset recipes.

My especial thanks go to David Johnston for reading the first two chapters and making such helpful comments. I am also indebted to Richard Cavendish, Andrew Butcher and Christopher Newberry for reading and advising on the rest of the book.

Lastly but not least, many thanks to Gloria Filbee for typing the manuscript.

Introduction

This book is a search for the unknown housewife in history. The unknown soldier has left his mark in the history books in the battles he fought, the weapons he used, the fortifications he built and the changes he brought about. But what about his wife, mother, sister, daughter? What was she doing while he was thus occupied? Whatever was happening in the outside world, she had to go on feeding, clothing and caring for her family, to the best of her ability, and in this way providing basic stability to the lives of ordinary people. Where did she live, what did she do, how did she manage, what aids did she have to doing her work?

It is thought that the earliest sowers of seeds to produce food crops and plants were most probably women. The relief of settling in one place with a little home grown food when tribes ceased to be nomadic must have been very great. The constant search for food, whether berries or grain, or on relying on what her husband managed to bring home for supper cannot have been conducive to a settled home life, as any modern weekend fisherman's wife will know. It was a great step forward when the first crops were grown and the first animals domesticated, for only then were the beginnings of civilization seen and the first permanent homes built. While she may have had little say in the type of home built, all the evidence shows that many of the improvements, alterations and redecorations to the home were carried out at the instigation of women, very often at the time of marriage or the birth of a child.

When we consider the places in which she has had to live throughout history woman has certainly had her ups and downs; from the top of an ancient hill-fort down to the villas and halls of the Romans and Saxons, from the top of a castle tower to the single or two storey levels of the homes of the succeeding centuries, until someone decided to put her up in the world again at the top of a block of high-rise flats, and always she has coped.

She has coped with producing the next generation with unfailing regularity, coped with washing, either more or less, according to the age in which she lived, and coped with cooking whatever food man has provided. She has clothed her family in whatever materials were at hand or, if they weren't at hand, produced garments from her own spun thread, gathered from whatever animals or plants were available. Until recently she has done much of this in a poor light, with an ever-present water problem and a constant fuel problem.

The energy crisis was with her for centuries and it looks as if she has now to deal with it again.

Her cries for help or of despair have been many times drowned by anything from the machines of war to the television. From time to time they have been answered by the provision of a variety of utensils with a greater or lesser degree of labour saving.

Today the assumptions of the past that running the home and bringing up the children is chiefly her responsibility are being increasingly questioned, not least by women themselves. There are signs everywhere that some of her traditional duties are being shared and re-allocated to enable her to live an independent life outside the home. Up to the point where we leave her, however, in the early years of this century, the acceptance of these duties as her natural role in life was unquestioned by ordinary women and it is a matter of fact, whether she liked it or not, that a woman's place *was* in the home.

My intention in this book is to pay tribute to those unknown housewives throughout history who, whatever the conditions, whatever the surroundings, whatever the weapons they used, have always managed.

Marjorie Filbee

The Roman Villa

No modern labour saving device has yet been invented which quite takes the place of a slave

The comfort and indeed luxury
which the lady of the villa enjoys
in this sentimental Victorian
painting were maintained by the
household slaves
A SILENT GREETING: Alma Tadema
(*Courtesy Tate Gallery*)

She sat at her dressing table, fastening delicate gold earrings in her ears and contemplating her appearance in her mirror (page 13.1). She was completing her toilette before the evening meal, which was always the high spot of her day.

This lady of Roman Britain enjoyed a standard of living far above that of either her Celtic sister 300 years before or her Anglo-Saxon counterpart 300 years later. Here in the 3rd century AD most people endured the same hard life as their forefathers, but her own position was very different.

She belonged to the small, privileged élite who lived in villas on large country estates in southern England. Her husband was a Briton whose aristocratic ancestors had been quick to adopt Roman ways, and his position kept her in the luxury to which she was accustomed. He was a councillor and magistrate and much concerned with local politics, harvest prospects and the affairs of his tenant farmers. When not hunting, he often visited the nearby town, where much of his time was spent at those centres for Roman gossip and scandal, the barber's and the municipal baths.

A bath before dinner

Taking a bath was an elaborate and an important procedure for both men and women, especially before dinner. The lady of the villa would leave her clothes in a dressing room and rest in the tepidarium (warm room); then she would stay for a while in the calidarium (hot room), and end her bath with a cold plunge. Her slave would be waiting to massage her with perfumed oils, to help her dress and to arrange her hair. A bath unit like this was usual in such a home. Sanitation was almost as important to upper-class Romans as it is to us today, and they even had lavatories which flushed.

Central heating was also considered a necessity in a modern home of the 3rd century. The 'hypocaust' system of heating consisted of pillars under the floor around which hot air circulated from an outside furnace. Concealed flues carried the heat up the walls and sometimes even over the vaulted ceiling.

The lady's comfort and security was further increased by glass in her windows, a momentous step forward in history. Many of the windows had exterior iron grilles and often shutters as well. After the Romans had left Britain it was not until the reign of Henry VIII in the 16th century that Englishmen again got around to putting much glass in windows. In medieval times it was a great luxury, reserved for only a few of the most important windows in the manor house.

Apart from the warmth of her home, the lady enjoyed one other valuable luxury: an abundance of slaves to assist her. No modern labour-saving device has yet been invented which quite takes the place of a slave. She addressed her slaves in Celtic, although she herself spoke fluent Latin with a slight provincial accent. She could also read and write Latin, but not without difficulty.

A personal slave would have been of particular help in contriving whatever intricate arrangements of waves, plaits, curls and ringlets were popular at the time. She could copy the latest styles from portraits of the empresses of Rome which appeared on coins in daily use. Such importance was attached to the hair styles of these leaders that their statues in Rome were sometimes made with detachable hair, enabling the coiffure to be altered as the fashion changed.

In the more elaborate styles false hair pieces were used. As the Roman poet Ovid remarked:

A woman flaunts in yards of purchased curls;
Failing her own, she buys another girl's.

The false hair pieces and wigs were made from the hair of German slave girls, from black hair imported from India, and from blond hair made by bleaching with sapo, a mixture of goat's fat and beech ash.

In contrast to their hair and jewellery Romano-British ladies wore the simple

1

2

13.1 Silver mirror,
found at Wroxeter,
the Roman city of
Viriconium, 3rd
century AD
(*Rowley's House
Museum, Shrewsbury*)

13.2 Disc brooch, 2nd
century AD (*page 14*)

14.1 Glass jars for
cosmetics, 2nd
century AD

14.2 Bronze strigil
with enamelled
handle 16.5 cm
(6½ in) long
(*Rockbourne Museum*)

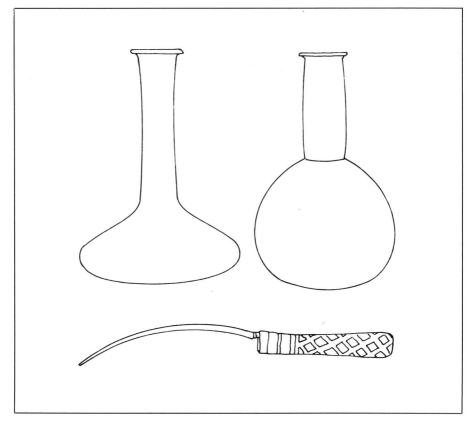

Roman tunics and cloaks, which had changed very little over a thousand years of the Republic and Empire. It comes as something of a surprise to realize that when it came to dress the Roman Empire was more or less held together with safety pins. These pins and brooches, called 'fibulae', were so well made that the springs in many of them still work after being buried for 1700 years. They were used to fasten the cloaks and tunics, and a woman made changes in her appearance by the different ways she pinned these garments and in the varying designs of her brooches.

If she ventured out on a hot summer's day in her own garden she could have a fan to keep her cool, a parasol, and even a leather bikini. Out of doors in public women wore cloaks, and draped these over their heads; they were not expected to appear bareheaded. Leather sandals were worn, and perhaps knitted stockings too, in the cold British climate, although with heated floors sandals might have been sufficient in the home.

Roman beauty aids

Many brooches were decorated with enamel work and were in the shape of animals and birds – a hare, a tortoise or a dolphin. There were disc brooches with glass bosses, very modern in appearance (13.2); other brooches were worn in pairs joined by a short silver chain. In the early days of the Roman Republic the wearing of jewellery had been frowned on, but by the time the Empire was at its height and the Romans had occupied Britain, luxury was in full swing. A rich

lady in Roman Britain would have worn a great deal of jewellery, with a large variety of both imported and home-produced designs from which to choose.

Her finished coiffure might be decorated with a jewelled hair net. Bone hair pins were of the same size and design as the plastic ones used by hairdressers today. The more elaborate pins, also used for fastening clothes, had heads decorated with jet, silver or pearls and with busts of goddesses and empresses. Necklaces were used to hang charms on much as bracelets are today.

Rings were in endless variety: gold, silver, bronze and jet, set with semi-precious and precious stones. There were betrothal rings engraved with two clasped hands. But a woman had to face the fact that when it came to rings her husband probably outdid her. His rings were larger and he wore more of them.

Her beauty aids were numerous and were contained in an array of little jars of glass or alabaster (14.1), with a small oblong stone palette on which to mix them. She used chalk and white lead to whiten her skin, red ochre for lipstick and rouge and powdered antimony or ashes for darkening her eyebrows. These were applied with glass rods, or small bronze or bone palette knives.

With her bath oil and strigil (14.2), a bronze scraper to remove dirt and oil after her bath, her tooth powder made of horn, perfumes, comb, tweezers, a mirror of polished bronze and her manicure implements, the personal clutter of her dressing table must have been quite impressive. In fact she rivalled the modern Eleanor Rigby

15 Dining room of the 3rd century AD, a reconstruction (*page 16*) (*Museum of London*)

16 Mosaic floor from Sparsholt Roman Villa, 3 m (about 9 ft 9 in) square (*Winchester City Museum*)

in the Beatles' song, with 'her face that she keeps in a jar by the door', for one Roman writer wrote of his Galla who lay at night 'stored away in a hundred caskets'. However, her husband was unlikely to complain about the time she took over her extensive toilette. He himself probably took longer.

Talking of inflation . . .

Eventually the diners would make their way to their couches in the dining room, the women perhaps hoping that the conversation that evening would not be too serious. This was Britain after nearly three hundred years of Roman occupation, and the men were likely to discuss current problems: the division of Britain into several provinces, increasing taxation, purchase tax, inflation, and now wage freezes and price controls. Life was by no means secure. Counterfeit money was in circulation, rural districts were threatened by unrest, and the coasts were being increasingly harried by Irish, Pict and Saxon raiders.

The Emperor Diocletian had threatened death or exile for those who disobeyed the new rules, but no one expected this to work. Anyway, there was no need to worry tonight. The food prepared by the slaves smelled excellent and the meal was to be eaten in a small, attractive and very colourful room. Although it was quite usual to sit up at the table on chairs or couches (15), many Britons had quickly become Romanized and adopted the 'triclinium', a room with couches which ran round three sides of a dining table and on which people reclined at meals.

Mosaic floors were laid even in small villas, and are found in a great variety of designs. These floors were composed of small pieces of coloured stone ('tesserae'), arranged in patterns and pictures on a concrete base. The villa at Sparsholt in Hampshire, a simple one-storey building of eight rooms with a verandah, was probably the home of a well-to-do gentleman farmer of the 3rd or 4th centuries, and it had mosaic floors of a high standard (16). The one in the main reception room was probably made of local materials except for the bright blue stones in the corner fans, which were perhaps imported.

At Sparsholt conventional motifs in black, white, red, blue and brown were used. The lady of the villa (17) probably had a book of designs from which to choose mosaics just as if she were choosing wallpaper today. Many designs were chosen for religious reasons; others have birds, animals or hunting scenes. Sea scenes with water nymphs and pictures featuring Orpheus were very popular.

The bright rooms made a fitting setting for the 'Sunday best' tableware found in so many English villas and throughout the Roman Empire. This was the glossy, dark red Samian ware decorated with elaborate designs (18), imported from Gaul in the first two centuries AD, before good British-made pottery could compete, and it is obvious from the many remains found that it was something every Romano-British housewife had to have in her home. Local potteries made a wide variety of pottery and cooking utensils for everyday use, each producing its own characteristic wares.

As has always been the case, the type of dinner ware varied with the wealth of the family. The highest quality and craftsmanship was available to those who could afford it: some very fine and well-preserved 4th-century silverware was found at Mildenhall in Suffolk. It includes dishes – one nearly 60 centimetres (2 feet) in diameter weighing about 8.2 kilogrammes (roughly 18¼ pounds), platters, bowls, goblets, and also two christening spoons, one with the inscription 'Papittedo Vivas' ('Long life to Papittedo') and one with a similar inscription to Pascentia.

If a household could not run to silver dishes, pewter ware (21.1) was a cheaper substitute, and many objects in bluish–green glass were imported from Gaul and the Rhineland.

To give us an idea of the great variety of food eaten in Roman Britain we have a collection of recipes by one Apicius, a sort of Roman Mrs Beeton of the first century AD. These recipes have been translated by Barbara Flower and Elizabeth Rosenbaum, two brave ladies who tried out the recipes to make sure the translations were as accurate as possible. There are recipes for sausages, rissoles, lamb, pork, beef, goose, duck and chicken, but there are also recipes for many ways of cooking crane, partridge, turtle dove and wood-pigeon; thrush, fig-pecker, peacock, pheasant, boar, venison, wild goat, hare and even dormice. The latter were to be stuffed with

17 The Sparsholt lady, from a wall painting of the 4th century AD, now in Winchester City Museum (*Department of the Environment*)

18 Samian ware bowl,
2nd century AD
(*British Museum*)

minced pork, as well as the minced meat of whole dormice which had been pounded with pepper, pine-kernels, asafoetida and liquamen. They were then to be sewn up and placed on a tile in the oven to cook.

Highly seasoned dishes

Liquamen was used in very many of the recipes. It was made in factories from small fish such as sprats and anchovies. It seems to have been used instead of salt, rather as we use Worcester sauce. Several towns were famous for their liquamen and in the ruins of Pompeii was found what could have been 'this week's special offer', a small jar with the inscription 'Best strained liquamen. From the factory of Umbricus Agathopus'.

Several recipes include built-in digestive and health aids. The Romans were advised to dress lettuce with vinegar and a little liquamen to make it more digestible and to prevent flatulence. It is doubtful if it was only lettuce that caused the indigestion, for there are so many recipes for sauces in the book that it seems well-to-do Romans ate very little plain food; every-thing was flavoured with spices, herbs, oil, wine and a great deal of honey.

The meal commenced with a libation, an offering of wine in sacrifice by the head of the house. The gustatio or first course was accompanied by mulsum, wine sweetened with honey. It was very similar to a first course today: an egg dish, salad or shellfish. Oysters were eaten in large quantities, judging by the number of oyster shells that have been found on villa sites in Britain. The fercula, or main course, may have consisted of several dishes, cut up with a knife and eaten with the fingers as forks were unknown, and last came the dessert of fresh or dried fruit, pastries and sweets. Music and entertainment followed according to the wealth of the family.

No doubt through all this the slaves were working away in the kitchen until a late hour. In a kitchen of a villa the size of Rockbourne in Hampshire with over 70 rooms, it must have taken many hands to cope with the amount of food needed, but the kitchen there does not seem to have been all that big for the task. Situated at the end of a passage away from the dining room, it had a doorway with a self-closing device, operated by pulley and weight, so that the turmoil of the kitchen did not disturb the peace of the dining room.

The photograph (19) shows a model reconstruction of the kind of kitchen found in humbler homes of the period. The cooking was done on a gridiron (20) or tripod (21.3) on a raised cooking hearth with charcoal underneath for fuel.

For baking or roasting a beehive-shaped oven was used, very like the cloam ovens in use in the west of England until recent times. It was heated by wood or charcoal burned inside, the meat or bread being put in to cook after raking out the ashes.

The wives of small farmers no doubt prepared much of the food themselves, perhaps with the help of one slave if they were lucky. Their days were fully occupied with home and family, and they lived a life very different from that of the wealthy villa dwellers. Mosaic floors, central heating and bath units were only added to their homes over the years if their farms prospered.

The shapes and sizes of cooking pots and dishes found all over Britain show the great variety of food that must have been served. There are sets of 'oven to table ware' dishes in graduated sizes (21.2), frying pans, skillets (21.4), sieves, colanders (22.1), and cheese presses. One of

19 Model of a Roman kitchen equipped with models of objects found at Silchester, 2nd century AD (*Reading Museum*)

the mortars (22.2) found at Silchester near Reading still contained remains of the fruit pulp (cherry and plum) last crushed in it, the basis of a Roman fruit fool perhaps.

The large number of cooking-pot remains found on villa sites suggests that while they were cheap and plentiful they were also difficult to clean, as the pottery was so coarse. Apicius starts many of his recipes by telling the cook to 'take a new pan'. After cooking and mixing highly seasoned foods it was probably easier, cheaper and safer to throw the pot away and start with a new one, if the strong flavour was not to penetrate the next dish. This, combined with the remains of pottery beehives (22.3) found at Rockbourne from which the honey was extracted by the simple process of breaking the pot, leads one to think that the 'disposable age' possibly started a little earlier than we realize.

The Roman writer, the elder Pliny, advised the growing of lemon balm in the garden to keep bees happy and to enable them to find their way home if they had strayed, an important consideration when honey played such a large part in the diet. But there were many other herbs in a Roman garden. There was no plain boiled cabbage for the Romans. It was cooked with cumin, salt, old wine and oil, pepper, lovage, mint, rue and coriander. They also used borage, chervil, chives, marjoram, savory, thyme and mallow. One Roman cook complained that some cooks served up 'whole pickled meadows'; they 'thrust herbs at you, then proceed to season those herbs with other herbs'.

The earliest gardens were of herbs and vegetables, much the same as those grown today, with artichokes, asparagus, beans, beetroot, cabbage, carrots, celery, cucumbers, marrows, leeks, lettuce, chicory, onions and turnips. Later the Roman love of formal gardens was adopted by the

20 Gridiron found at Silchester, 2nd century AD *(page 19)* *(Reading Museum)*

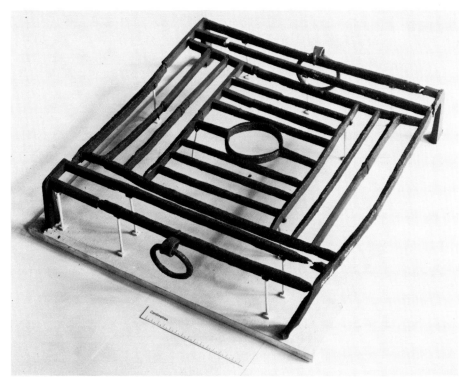

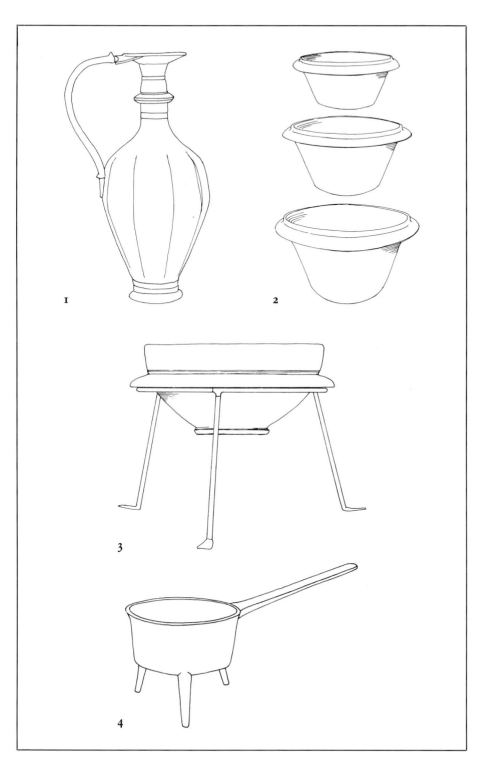

1

2

3

4

21.1 Pewter flagon found in Sussex, 4th century AD (*page 17*) (*British Museum*)

21.1 Pewter flagon found in Sussex, 4th century AD (*page 17*) (*British Museum*)

21.2 Three New Forest 'oven to tableware' dishes, in graded sizes, 3rd century AD (*page 19*) (*Rockbourne Museum*)

21.3 New Forest ware bowl, showing how it would have stood on a tripod stand, 3rd century AD (*page 19*) (*Rockbourne Museum*)

21.4 Bronze skillet of a type in use since Roman times (19th century) (*page 19*)

22.1 Pottery colander,
3rd century AD
(*page 19*)

22.2 Mortar, from
Silchester, 2nd
century AD (*page 20*)
(*Reading Museum*)

22.3 Pottery beehive,
3rd century AD, 52 cm
(1 ft 8½ in) high
(*page 20*)
(*Rockbourne Museum*)

Romanized Britons, helped by skilled designers who travelled round the provinces. The lady of the villa would have looked out on to a very formal garden, with well-defined paths and drives, flower beds of symmetrical designs, and hedges and trees that were never allowed to stay as nature intended.

The success of a Roman garden was judged by the intricacy of the topiary work on its trees, and the amount of man-made stonework and statuary and number of fountains. The excavation of the garden of the Roman palace at Fishbourne, near Chichester in Sussex, unearthed the bedding trenches which had been cut into the clay and gravel soil and filled with a carefully marled loam, enabling plants to grow on land which would otherwise have been infertile: work done by knowledgeable and careful gardeners of 1900 years ago. The water pipes that fed the marble basins and fountains of the garden still lay in position, and parts of the marble basins were found.

There were also holes for posts which probably supported climbing plants. The elder Pliny mentions planting roses in kitchen debris, and trenches in front of the east wing of Fishbourne Palace had been filled with kitchen waste, so roses no doubt grew there, introduced by the Romans. Not everything in the garden was lovely. From seeds found at Silchester we know that the gardener there had to cope with bindweed, brambles, docks, nettles and deadly nightshade.

The younger Pliny vividly describes the gardens at his homes outside Rome, and among the plants that gave him pleasure were acanthus, box hedges, rosemary, vines, mulberries and figs. The terrace was scented with violets and at Tuscany there was an outdoor pool for dining in the open, the main courses being served on the marble edge, with the lighter dishes floating on the water in vessels shaped like birds or little boats. Whether the English climate allowed such a style of outdoor living we do not know, for during the

Roman occupation the weather became progressively wetter. The indoor rooms with their frescos of flowers, trees, fruit and foliage were probably used more often.

When night fell on the villa it was lit by small lamps of pottery or bronze (23), with a hole for the wick and a hole to replenish the oil. No doubt in poorer homes the wick burned in a shell or hollow stone, but the enclosed lamp must have given a better light with less smoke. The lamps are found in a great variety of designs, some with several wicks, and filling them and trimming the wicks must have been a never-ending chore. Candles were also used, in pottery candlesticks or in iron candle holders.

The lady of the house would eventually transfer herself from her couch in the dining room to another couch in her bedroom. Perhaps a mattress was placed on a chest or masonry support, with cushions and bedclothes for comfort, but in general the family and guests simply bedded down on daytime couches or on mattresses on the floor in any convenient room.

Homespun clothes

If the evening in the villa was elaborate, the morning was simple. Breakfast was not a formal meal, and consisted of bread or fruit with a drink of water. Clothes were few and uncomplicated. Under her outer tunic of wool or linen a woman wore an undertunic with elbow-length sleeves over a band of linen round her bust. If she was married her tunic was longer and more voluminous than a young girl's.

The material was spun or woven by herself or by her slaves on a wooden spindle which had a pottery, bone or metal weight on the end. This circular ring or whorl held the spindle in position, and rotated as the thread was pulled out from the wool to be spun and wound onto the spindle: a method used for several thousand years.

The spun thread was then woven on

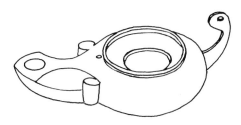

23 Roman lamp, 2nd century AD (*British Museum*)

looms, either in the home or, if the home was quite near a town, perhaps in a workshop. The distinctive British duffel-coat and blankets were famous throughout the Roman Empire.

If women were much occupied in making cloth, little sewing was required of them, pins and brooches taking the place of seams. Some sewing or embroidery must have been done, as thimbles have been found, including a small child's thimble at Rockbourne. Decorated fringes are shown on some tunics, and needles were of bone or bronze and were blunt and coarse. Scissors resembled small iron shears.

Collecting water from the well must have been a continual chore, as must the grinding of corn for the daily bread in a handmill or quern, or in large mills turned by slaves, donkeys or blindfolded horses. Brown and white loaves were baked; but even so long ago there were those who advocated wholemeal bread and thought it gave added strength and aided the digestion.

Lunch was also a light snack, so there was plenty of time during the day for the domestic work of the household. There were baskets to be woven and also the children to be looked after, the older ones being instructed by a tutor who was usually a Greek slave. Many children's toys have been found: dolls, model chariots and the counters and dice from endless games. There is a small folded beaker (24.1) of New Forest pottery too small for drinking from, but the right size for shaking a dice. The remains of a pottery games board have been found; it looks as though it was used for an early form of

24.1 New Forest
ware dice pot,
9 cm (3½ in) high
(*page 23*)
(*Rockbourne Museum*)

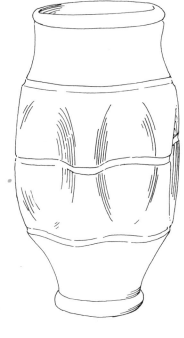

24.2 Child's feeding
cup, 3rd century AD,
7 cm (2¾ in) high
(*Rockbourne Museum*)

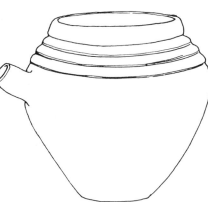

backgammon. There is a baby's feeding cup (24.2) at Rockbourne in New Forest pottery, the forerunner of the plastic cups in use today, and a Samian ware feeding cup (25) has been found in Colchester.

The household slaves

How irksome all these domestic duties were for a woman would depend as always on how much help she had. Slaves were a form of property and their owners controlled their marriages and the disposal of their children – who were automatically slaves like their parents. But they could be freed, and the relations between masters and slaves in Roman Britain were not always unpleasant. Slaves were often skilled workers and able to rise in the household hierarchy. Masters were prevented by law from casting off their slaves when they became ill or too old to work. Their skills and work were appreciated and rewarded by their owners, as can be seen from inscriptions on the tombstones which are the only record of their lives.

Religion came high on the list of matters to be attended to during the day. In early times there were many gods to be served, especially the household gods in the shrine or lararium set aside in the home in their honour. Small figures of these gods in bronze or clay stood in these shrines and most probably included Venus or Juno Lucina, the goddess of childbirth, sitting in a basket chair nursing a baby, and Minerva the patroness of the arts and of, among other things, spinning and weaving.

In the Corinium Museum at Cirencester is a stone relief showing three mother goddesses (deae matres) holding fruit and loaves, symbols of fertility. These goddesses were widely revered, whether portrayed in groups of three or as individuals, again seated in the same type of chair, or accompanied by three small male godlets wearing hooded cloaks.

In AD 312 Christianity was made the official religion of the Roman Empire, and several signs of the gradual spread of Christianity have been found in the villas

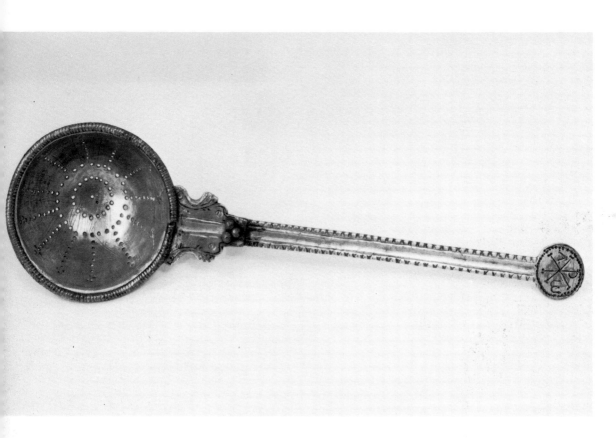

of England. The Chi-Rho monogram (the first two letters of the name of Christ in Greek) is found on many stones and plates. A silver strainer with this monogram is illustrated (26). At the villa in Lullingstone in Kent there is a room decorated with Christian wall paintings, which may have been a private chapel. At Hinton St Mary a mosaic floor, now in the British Museum, has what is thought to be an early representation of Christ incorporated in its design. At Rockbourne a milestone dedicated to the Emperor Trajan Decius, a persecutor of the Christians in the third century, was found placed face downwards and used as a step, possibly by the Christian inhabitants of the villa.

As to the diseases that led the Romans to their tombs, these were much the same as today: chest troubles, pneumonia and heart disease, but also leprosy. Their skeletons show little sign of faulty nutrition, but arthritis was common. Their teeth were often not so much decayed as very worn down, probably due to the amount of grit in their diet, (in, for instance, stone-ground bread). Most of their illnesses were treated with herbs and blood-letting and that they did make good recoveries is shown by the thanksgiving offerings found in shrines associated with healing.

Pliny was full of advice for every ailment, including a hot application of turnips to cure chilblains, probably a common complaint of British Romans. Small solid sticks of eye-salves had to be dissolved by the patient in egg white, sweet wine or water. Square stone slabs inscribed with the maker's name were used by oculists to mark cakes of eye ointment. One such stone has 'Unbeatable, a preparation of aniseed or dill' on one side in Latin.

One can only hope that a woman did not often suffer pain as anaesthetics were few; a decoction of poppy, henbane and mandrake hardly seems sufficient to deaden the pain of a surgical operation. The rate of infant mortality was high, and sadly her own life expectancy was also quite short.

However, as the lady of the villa took her bath before dinner she was, no doubt, healthy and happy and convinced that the Empire would last forever. Yet her way of life would not be known again for 1700 years – by then we had run out of slaves.

CHOOSING (detail):
J. W. Godward
(*Roy Miles Gallery*:
Rodney Wright-Watson)

The Anglo-Saxon Hall

Outside was a wild and dangerous countryside; inside the food was accompanied by stories of valiant deeds, told in words set to harp and lyre

Saxon noble receiving guests in his hall, as imagined by a 19th-century artist
(*Mansell Collection*)

The lady of the Anglo-Saxon hall knew nothing of the easy life in Roman Britain five centuries earlier. The ruins of the great stone villas remained, but she thought that giants had built them. In any case she was much too busy to worry about ancient history.

Her lord and his retainers would soon pour into the small wooden hall in which they all lived. They would be ravenous and thirsty after their day's work, and she and her daughters must be ready to serve them with the evening meal.

Feasting and song within

The hall was warmed by the great wood fire burning on a stone hearth in the middle of the earth floor, and she had scattered clean rushes over the floor to absorb the mud the men would soon bring in. She needed to keep a watchful eye on the fire, and make sure the rushes were kept at a safe distance, as fire was an ever-present hazard.

Her husband's life was largely devoted to turning the forest clearings into the ploughed fields, meadows, farmsteads and villages that still shape our countryside today. Whatever his wealth or position he was first and foremost a farmer and she was a farmer's wife. Wrestling with nature in its raw state must have been a full-time occupation. Quite apart from the routine work of clearing, planting and harvesting, there were the storms and tempests to cope with, and crop failures and plagues that affected men, women, children and beasts. Keeping the wolf from the door was an actuality, not an idle saying.

The Venerable Bede, writing in the 8th century AD, incidentally gives us a rather pertinent picture of the life of Anglo-Saxons in their hall houses. He quotes an Anglo-Saxon nobleman who compares the life of man to the flight of a sparrow. 'In winter', he says, 'when men are sitting in their feasting hall, a sparrow, seeing the light, flies in through the one door, across the lighted room, and out through the other door, into the darkness and storms outside. In the same way, man comes from darkness, passes through a brief period of light and then returns to darkness.'

The first point that strikes one is that life was often short. We also see clearly that there were two opposite doors in the hall, one on each side, and that even in winter they were likely to be open. The third point is that birds were probably flying round the dining tables. Continuing their feasting and fun in these conditions shows the hardiness of the Anglo-Saxon ladies and their unconcern with material comforts, enabling them to take all this in their stride as many countrywomen have done ever since.

When darkness came and work outdoors had to cease, the companionship and warmth of the communal hall, combined with plenty of food and drink, must have been very welcome and well earned. Outside was a wild and dangerous countryside; inside the food was accompanied by stories of valiant deeds both of the past and of the present, told in words set to harp and lyre. As the farming was so often accompanied by fighting and feuding, with both neighbours and enemies, there was no shortage of material for the evenings' entertainment. The type of lyre that might have accompanied the songs is illustrated (31). It was of maple wood with pegs of poplar or willow and was of expert craftsmanship.

Games were also played, with bone gaming pieces; chessmen made of whalebone dating from the 10th century have been found in Dorset. The children acted out the fierce songs they listened to with the aid of miniature battle-axes. They were encouraged to express themselves, without rebuke, to give them confidence. It is said that the young King Alfred at the age of nine could not read but committed to memory the Saxon poems he heard recited and repeated so many times.

The lady of the house and her daughters and servants prepared the meal and then served it, with cups of mead or ale handed first to her lord and husband and then to any guests. The farming background of the occupants of the hall is emphasized by the title 'lord', which is a compound word deriving from 'loaf ward' or 'loaf keeper', while 'lady' derives from 'loaf kneader', 'maker of bread'. This puts everyone in their place and shows the preoccupation with the staff of life of the early holders of these titles.

If there were servants to help they were probably 'serfs' or slaves. A woman could free her slaves if she wished and this 'manumitting' of slaves was later much encouraged by the Christian Church.

The hall was a rectangular building, probably about 15 metres by 8 metres (roughly 16 yards by 9 yards), with one end partitioned off to form a separate room, occasionally three rooms, perhaps the sleeping quarters for the lord and his family. So it is probable that the women of the family had a small private room to which to retire when the feasting and fun became too much. A recently excavated Saxon village at Chalton in Hampshire revealed the remains of smaller square houses around the main hall which may have been the burs or bowers where sons or young men slept, or where women lived.

Timber was plentiful, as so much of the dense forest that covered the country had to be cleared, but excavations have shown that even kings and wealthy lords lived in what were little more than large barns. The floors were probably of earth, but were sometimes cobbled with flints, stones and animal bones.

Furniture must have been at a minimum, due not to lack of wood but to lack of space. Seating was on wooden benches fixed round the walls, and boards were set up on trestles when meals were served, then taken down again at the end of the day, so that the servants and dogs could sleep on the floor around the fire. The smoke escaped through the blackened timbers and thatch of the roof as best it could. (Perhaps this is why the doors were open.) There may have been a hole in the

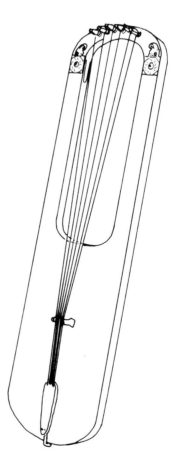

31 Anglo-Saxon lyre, reconstructed from remains at the Sutton Hoo Ship burial, 7th century AD (*British Museum*)

roof but too fierce an updraught would have been likely to draw sparks into the thatch.

The smoke rising upwards would both keep the thatch free from bugs and cure the meat and skins hanging from the rafters. In crofters' homes in Scotland (32), if rain managed to percolate through the straw thatch roofs it mixed with the soot inside and fell in great black drops, known as 'soot drip', onto the occupants below.

Lighting would have been by torches stuck in the walls or by rushlights and candles for those who could afford them. King Alfred found that church candles blew out easily in the draughts and had lanterns made of wood and white ox-horn; oil-burning lamps were also used.

32 Central peat fire burning at a
farmhouse in the Isle of Lewis
(*National Museum of Antiquities,
Scotland*)

Most of the cooking, especially of the roasted meat, would be done out of doors away from the hall, because of the ever-present danger of fire, but no doubt in bad weather a cauldron over the central fire had to suffice, and there would be stew once again that night. In poorer homes this would be all that was possible, and it would be a meatless stew at that. The possession of a kitchen was a status symbol and one way to move up in the complex Saxon world where there were many degrees of class. A man who had five hides of land and a church, who was also entitled to a place in the King's hall and also had a kitchen, could call himself a thane. Of course, life was not the same throughout the Saxon period. In the 5th century the Saxons were pagans invading a Christian land; in the 10th century they had become Christians defending themselves against Viking invaders. Conditions of housing also varied from region to region and from class to class.

In the smaller one-room halls the domestic animals lived in the end portion, all under one roof with the family, as in many poor homes before and since. Many Saxon peasants lived in very small huts, and there are Saxon skeletons with abnormally worn ankle bones, caused, it has been surmised, by too much squatting.

How the Saxons dined

Obviously bread formed an important part of the diet, but stock raising, especially of sheep, was important, so that meat must have been eaten frequently by those who could afford it. Dairy produce and the milk from ewes were also used.

There are large quantities of deer bones on the site at Chalton, indicating that when not farming the Saxons there were busy out hunting. When fresh domestic meat was in short supply during the winter months this must have helped to keep meat on the menu. The forests and streams of England were full and free at this time, and the penal laws of the Normans were still to come. Stag hunting, fox hunting and

hawking were favourite pastimes; hunting dogs were prized possessions, useful also for clearing up the food remains in the hall.

As well as being smoked, meat was preserved for use during the winter months with salt, an important commodity brought to the home by pedlars. Before the Norman conquest England was famous for beef, bacon and wheaten cakes, and for its 'small ale' or 'single ale' made from barley, although wine was imported and drunk by the wealthy. There were plentiful supplies of butter and cheese. Dealing with the dairy produce and making the beer would be women's work, along with the preservation of meat.

The dishes on which the food was served were usually of heavy, coarse, hand-made pottery. Wheel-thrown pottery of the kind made in Roman Britain did not appear again in any great quantity until the 9th century. There seem to have been pottery workshops which sold their wares over large areas. High-quality domestic ware, hard and burnished, has been found at a large excavated village at West Stow in Suffolk.

The heavy pottery of the Saxon dining table was offset by the high quality of the glass vessels used, both imported from the Continent and made in Britain. The beakers were often cone-shaped (33),

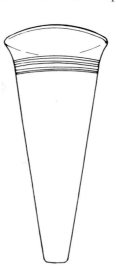

33 Glass beaker, 6th century AD (*Bury St Edmunds*)

34 Rhenish glass claw
beaker found in Castle
Eden, Durham
(5th–6th century AD)
(*British Museum*)

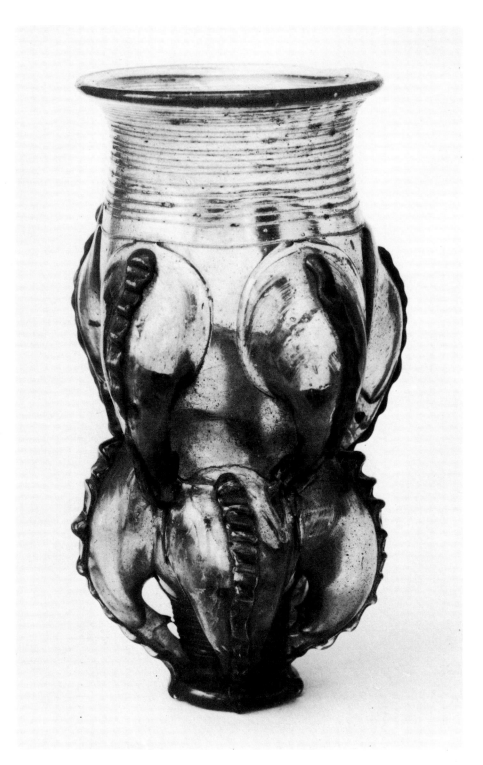

and as they could not stand on the table, the drink had to be quaffed in one go and the glass then laid down on its side; drinks were not delicately sipped in Saxon times. Some of the beakers found in women's graves in a Saxon cemetery at Mucking in Essex are very ornate. Many were of a much earlier age than the women with whom they were buried and must have been passed on from one generation to another as valued objects.

The claw beaker illustrated (34) demonstrates exceptional technical skill. Each 'claw' of hollow glass was blown out from the body of the vessel so that liquid flowed into the claws emphasizing their translucent effect. It contrasts strangely with the heavy domestic pottery of the time. Horn beakers and drinking horns were also used.

Coping with the washing

One thing the Saxon wife did not spend her time doing was taking baths, for there were no baths or drains and all water had to be fetched from the well or the nearest stream. Many Saxon villages were built near a stream or river which obviously played an important part in the lives and religious beliefs of the people. Springs, as well as trees, stones and rocks were among the things to which a Christian archbishop forbade the giving of votive offerings.

Laundry was probably dealt with, if at all, in these streams (35.1). A decree of AD 827 forbade women to make clothes, card wool, beat hemp or shear sheep on a Sunday, and it also forbade them to wash clothes in public on that day, giving a good indication of how their weekdays were occupied.

Living conditions were harsh, so a woman's clothes covered her well and kept out the draughts. She wore a kirtle or undergarment of linen or wool and a tunic that hung down to the ground. For extra warmth she might wear two tunics, with a girdle round her waist, the under tunic having long sleeves and the overdress having shorter and wider ones. Over these she wore a mantle rather like a poncho. Her dress was often decorated with bands of weaving or embroidery and in East Anglia her cuffs might have been fastened with an elaborate bronze hook-and-eye fastening. A lady at her toilette is illustrated (35.2).

Her head was covered with a silk or

35.1 Detail from print showing woman washing clothes in a stream (*British Museum*)

35.2 Detail from a manuscript showing a lady at her toilette (*British Museum and Weidenfeld and Nicolson Archives*)

linen wrap according to her means. From her girdle hung a variety of objects: a small bronze needle case, a double-sided bone comb, and a bronze girdle-hanger with imitation keys. This 'chatelaine' may have been a symbol of a woman's position, recognized in law, as keeper of the store room and storage chests. Her personal possessions were carried in a purse which had a bronze bar with a central loop to attach it to her girdle. A bronze work box is illustrated (36).

Her greatest outlet for artistic expression in dress was still her jewellery, as it had been in Roman times. Here she had a large choice of earrings, rings and armlets and of brooches, often worn in pairs, one on each shoulder, with necklaces that hung between them across her chest. The brooch illustrated (37.1) is 14 cm (5½ in) in length, of a square-headed type popular in the 6th century AD worn with the head downwards. There were gilded, saucer-shaped brooches and richly jewelled disc brooches (37.2). Some have gold filigree wire-ornament between the jewels and are

works of high craftsmanship such as the example shown (37.3) which depicts the five senses.

These possessions and her dresses were of such importance to a woman that they were often bequeathed in wills, including a note of their worth: 'a necklace of forty mancuses' or 'a brooch worth six mancuses'. A mancus would buy about three acres of land, so the jewellery was of some considerable value. When not disposed of in her will it often followed her to her grave. At the Saxon burial ground at Mucking in Essex many strings of amber and coloured glass beads were found, even in children's graves. Some had a large spindle whorl as a centrepiece, indicating the importance of spinning in a woman's life.

Taking it with her

It seems it was important for a woman in pagan Saxon times to be buried with her most intimate possessions to accompany her on her journey to the next life. In many cases this practice was continued even after

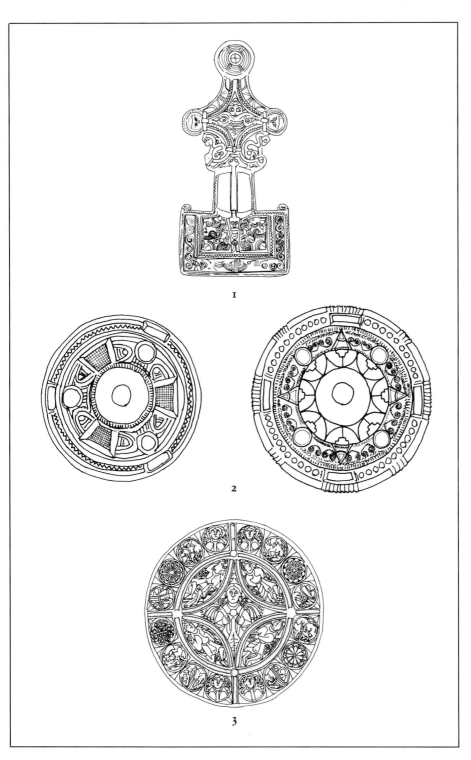

1

2

3

37.1 Anglo-Saxon
silver-gilt brooch
from Isle of Wight,
6th century AD
(*British Museum*)

37.2 Anglo-Saxon
jewelled disc-
brooches, from
Faversham, Kent,
6th–7th centuries AD
(*British Museum*)

37.3 Anglo-Saxon
disc-brooch depicting
the five senses,
9th century
(*British Museum*)

38 Spinning with the distaff in the Highlands in 1840, the same method being used by the Romans and Anglo-Saxons (*National Museum of Antiquities, Scotland*)

conversion to Christianity. A child might be buried with some old worn-out or patched articles that had probably belonged to her mother or grandmother, including festoons of beads much too big for her, a cracked brooch with its stones missing or a patched girdle-hanger.

One woman buried in Cambridgeshire wore a collar of silver pendants, had a bronze work-box hanging by a chain, a wooden box at her feet containing a bone comb, chalk beads and spindle whorls and a food offering of lamb chops. Amulets (charms against evil), such as pieces of rock, amber, amethyst or pebbles are found wrapped in linen and placed under a woman's head in her grave.

Apart from making clothes for herself and her family, the wife had to provide all the other comforts and decorations in the home. Cushions, pillows, mattresses, bed covers, seat covers and wall hangings were all made, spun and woven by the women of the family. From the decree of 827 it looks as if they also had to shear the sheep before they could get started on making a woollen garment. These furnishings were handed down from generation to generation and were prized possessions often featuring in women's wills. It was not unknown for a woman to hold lands on condition that she kept a church supplied with hangings.

By the end of the Saxon period English embroidery was the finest in Europe, particularly in church vestments, incorporating much colour and gold thread. William the Conqueror, on returning home after a visit to England, astonished his court with the quality of the garments he took back with him. An early Exeter book of gnomic verses lays down the aphorism that 'A woman's place is at her embroidery', although this was not the general view of a woman's position in Anglo-Saxon society. The equality she held with men was not achieved again for many centuries.

Curled hair and pointed nails
A description of the dress of 7th-century nuns by the learned cleric Aldhelm, who was protesting loudly at their appearance, is somewhat revealing both of himself and the nuns. They wore 'an undergarment of the finest cloth, a red or blue tunic, a head-dress and sleeves with silk borders; their shoes are adorned with red dyed skins; the locks on their temples and foreheads are crimped by the curlers. In the place of dark head coverings they wear white and coloured veils which hang down richly to the feet and are held in place by ribbons sewn on to them. Finger nails are sharpened like hawks' talons.' If this was the appearance of the nuns we can let our imaginations run riot as to the everyday wear of the wealthier farmer's wife.

Spindle whorls (38, 40) and loom weights abound in the remains of Anglo-Saxon settlements. Some huts appear to have been specially used for weaving. Wool was the commonest fabric woven, hence the importance of sheep-farming

from this time onwards and throughout the medieval period. It varied from fine quality cloth to a thick tweed-like material. The loom was a rectangular upright frame which often leaned against the wall of the house, the warps weighted down with baked clay rings tied to the ends. As the woven section grew it was wound over the top rail and the threads were 'beaten up' with wooden bars or swords and finer adjustments to the threads to tighten the weave were made with pointed bone pins.

Goats were among the domesticated animals kept and goats' hair was used for blankets, hoods and cloaks. Linen was quite common, woven from flax, and silk was used both for embroidery and as cloth by the wealthier members of society. Rich silks were imported from the East, as well as Byzantine silver, bronze bowls from Egypt, and ivory from Africa. Cowrie shells from tropical waters have been found in graves, emphasizing the wide trading connections of the Anglo-Saxons.

The Saxons regarded towns not so much as centres for living but as markets, where the agricultural produce of the surrounding countryside could be sold and where the farmers and their wives could purchase foreign luxury goods. There were few workshops in the towns, most goods being home-made in the countryside. The Saxon love of the country and nature is shown in all their art and this sense of line and colour was given further outlet for expression in Christianity. The vestments and church embroidery made by women, and the illuminated manuscripts of the monks, remain to show their high achievements in this respect.

The Church tried to make gradual changes from pagan Saxon beliefs to Christianity, but there is much evidence of the way in which earlier beliefs persisted. The only medicine known was a combination of magic and faith healing, rough surgery and bleeding. In the early centuries women placed their children on roofs or in ovens to heal fevers. Many charms have been found, written in the margins of books, against eye trouble and to help in childbirth and fertility, some employing elaborate rituals and a strange mixture of magical and Christian incantations. Others were to help against attacks by witchcraft and demons.

Three 'miserere me deus' and nine paternosters were to be sung while cutting nine bramble chips, which were to be boiled in milk, three doses of the resulting potion being a cure for dysentery. Honey being the main ingredient of mead and the only sweetening agent available there were also charms to help in catching a swarm of bees.

What a Saxon lady learned in church would have reinforced much of what she already believed, at the same time clashing with many of her pagan beliefs. Christianity stressed the sanctity of marriage and the home. The Saxons had always held the home and the family in high regard even if they did not so regard marriage. Saxon homesteads were probably family communities surrounded by an enclosure, defended against all comers.

But they were a practical people and regarded marriage not as a bond which could only be ended by death, but as a contract which could be broken by either party as the need arose. Too many harsh realities existed in their lives; there was even the possibility that one partner might be carried off into slavery, perhaps to another country, so it was difficult to persuade them that marriage was forever.

Rights of a Saxon woman

A woman's kinsmen arranged her marriage, with her consent, settled the terms of her marriage agreement and continued to look after her interests after her marriage. It was possible for her to own considerable property in her own right and to dispose of it freely. Many names of English villages and towns have the name of a Saxon woman incorporated in them. Wulfrun whose 'heah turn' or chief manor has become Wolverhampton lived in the 10th century. Goodwood in Sussex was Godgifu's wood. There are enough names of this kind to suggest that it was not unusual for a Saxon woman to own land.

40 Detail from the Luttrell Psalter, showing a woman feeding her chickens while spinning (*page 39*) (*British Museum and Weidenfeld and Nicolson Archives*)

Detail from a manu-
script showing
women ferreting
(*British Museum and
Weidenfeld and Nicolson
Archives*)

She was also capable of defending her property in the courts, or if necessary with an army. On the death of her husband her children stayed with her, while her family administered the property during the children's minority; she was allowed to make her own decision as to any second marriage, but her family was always behind her and she had the assurance that her honour and her rights would be upheld by the law.

The plain Saxon homes were gradually extended by extra rooms. Like their churches, by the end of the Saxon period some of these homes were being built in stone, becoming the foundation of the later medieval manor houses described in a later chapter.

The Castle

Firstly a military centre in a male-dominated society and secondly home for the nobleman's lady, her family and her women retainers

This detail from a religious
manuscript shows how a newborn
baby would be bathed in a castle
bedroom, while his mother looked
on (*page 46*)
(*British Museum*)

A woman living in a castle in the early years after the Norman conquest was likely to find herself either at the top of a wooden tower, itself on the top of a man-made mound or 'motte', or else in the bailey, the defended enclosure of the castle, in a hall not unlike the wooden hall with thatched roof of the Anglo-Saxons.

Gone was a woman's position in charge of the household; it was now run by men and for men. If she owned property, she could no longer deal with it herself as the free Saxon woman had; all her dispositions were subject to her husband's consent.

Her husband was unlikely to be the most popular figure in the district. He was an invader, and had probably demolished many of the local inhabitants' homes in building his castle. The mound at Oxford is said to have been piled on top of existing Saxon cottages; 166 houses were destroyed to build the castle at Lincoln and 113 at Norwich.

Many Norman noblemen were given several estates in England in the years after 1066, and spent their time travelling from one to the other. To defend their properties in a hostile land, from the people, from the King, and from each other, they built castles: wooden fortifications at first and later the massive stone fortresses we can still see today. In most cases stone buildings were not likely to have been built until some 30 years after the wooden ones, when the mound had settled enough to stand the weight of the huge structures to be erected. For this reason many castles took advantage of natural hill-tops, like the early castle at Bramber in Sussex in the south, or Edinburgh Castle in the north.

With the coming of the Normans the peak period for the defence of the aristocrat's home was reached. This is no doubt the reason that the only statement on housing generally known is that 'an Englishman's home is his castle'.

The castle, as well as being a military centre in a male-dominated society, was also home for the nobleman's lady, her family and her women retainers. Home improvements at this time ran along the lines of strengthening the walls and entrances and experimenting with variously shaped towers as defences against siege engines and mining. A large variety of more efficient arrow-loops were designed: those narrow slits in the walls through which the defenders could shoot at the enemy without being seen. Safety was considered more important than light, although in view of the fact that there was no glass in the windows this was probably an advantage. Staircases were steep and winding so that they could be more easily defended.

High level living

The whole structure was built of hard cold stone and it is difficult to think of it as a home in any sense of the word.

But a home it certainly was. One that, to use the words of V. Sackville-West when writing of Berkeley Castle in Gloucestershire (45), 'exacts a high level of living from the soul'. This high level of living many ladies of the past seem to have achieved.

The wooden tower was gradually replaced by a rectangular stone tower with walls anything up to 4.5 metres (15 feet) thick, and it was at the top of this that the women of the castle made a home.

The entrance was usually at first-floor level, with wooden or stone steps up to it. It often had an additional defence area built around it, all to make access as difficult as possible. The ground floor was without windows and was used to store the large quantity of supplies needed. It could only be reached by an internal stairway from the floor above.

The first floor might accommodate the garrison and perhaps the chapel. Usually the communal hall was on the next floor and above this were the living quarters of the lord and his family. The top floor was the only part of the tower that was considered safe enough to have slightly larger windows, giving it the name of the 'solar' or sun room. Somewhere in the

tower would be the wardrobe, not then a cupboard but a room or rooms where, as well as robes, spices, plate and jewels were stored.

The stone tower, which in time of trouble was the last refuge for the inhabitants of the castle and for everyone in the surrounding countryside, was known as the 'donjon', later to become 'dungeon'. As it was from time to time used as a prison, being the strongest part of the

castle, a dungeon came to mean a prison in the lower regions of a castle. Perhaps this was because prisoners were sometimes housed in the ground floor storage room to which there was no outside entrance. In fact many prisoners, often of royal blood and often female, did their languishing in the upper living quarters of the castle, perhaps for many years.

The word 'motte' (the mound on which the tower stood) was eventually applied to

45 Berkeley Castle with 12th century shell keep, built not on top of the mound but around it (*Aerofilms*)

the ditch round the mound, which became the 'moat', and in the 16th century the donjon became known as the 'keep'.

Hygiene was not as primitive in castles as might be supposed. There were latrines, 'garde-robes' or 'privies', built into the walls on each floor of the keep. They emptied into the moat, if there was one, or simply outside the wall, accumulating waste which needed to be buried at frequent intervals. During a siege of the castle when this could not be done the waste bred fevers and it was not unknown for a keep to be surrendered because the occupants were weakened in this way. Chamber pots appear in castle household accounts.

Unfortunately enemies were likely to climb up the latrine to get into the castle. Those whose job it was to keep the latrines clean were among the higher paid workers in the Middle Ages.

A well for fresh water was essential and usually in the basement, although water was not much used for drinking. There was often a shaft up through the thickness of the wall, which had a small arched opening on to each floor, where a bucket could be pulled up.

Baths could be taken in a wooden tub, rather like a half barrel, but heating and carrying the water for this obviously involved great effort. In fact Lady Mabel of Belesme, Countess of Shrewsbury, found it easier to bathe in the river, even in November; no doubt in peaceful times the nearby rivers were used for much washing of clothes and persons, as they had always been.

The only female servant in the castle apart from the children's nurses was the laundress, whose work looking after the household linen must have been very arduous but who was among the lowest paid workers in the castle. The lady's waiting-women, however, helped her to dress and with sewing and other tasks.

Bathing the baby
The upper classes in medieval castles probably had a higher standard of hygiene than in the centuries that followed. Monasteries set this high standard of cleanliness which would be copied by the many members of the nobility who stayed in them from time to time.

Medieval drawings show babies being bathed in wooden baths and even in a cauldron. As the water had probably been heated in this same cauldron over a fire. the easiest way was just to pop the baby in. It is said that the sickly infant son of Edward I had a gallon of wine added to his bath to strengthen him.

At Leeds Castle in Kent a rare bath chamber with a vaulted roof was built for Edward I in 1291. It has water 1.2 metres (4 feet) deep which comes in from the lake which surrounds the castle, through an inlet defended by a portcullis. It has a ledge and a recess for the bather, and there is a dressing-room above.

In the women's apartments no doubt a good deal of cooking was done in the fireplace, for children or for small meals. Cauldrons have changed little in design over hundreds of years and they could be

46 Medieval pot hanger

47 Cooking over a portable fire in a castle bedroom; the newborn baby is swaddled (*British Museum*)

hung on an iron hanger (46) of a type that has been in use until the present century. The height of the cauldron can be regulated on the ratchets.

Fireplaces are found in many living rooms of the keep, and those rooms not heated by a fireplace were probably heated by a portable brazier. One medieval drawing shows a woman heating food in a skillet over a portable fire in a bedroom (47). However, there are indications that some castle fires were only lit at early dawn or in the evening, in times of sickness or blood-letting, or for keeping young children warm.

The early fireplaces had stone hoods to contain the smoke as the fireplace recess was small. When fireplaces were carried deeper into the wall the hoods were not necessary and they diminished to a narrow mantelshelf.

A woman rising early for mass in a cold castle must have wanted clothes that were quickly slipped into, with no time spent on elaborate hairstyles. Her clothes were warm and draughtproof. She wore a gown with a round neck and long sleeves, and a girdle tied low at the waist with its ends hanging almost to the ground. Under this was an undergown and under that a camise or chemise, a shorter undergarment of white linen or silk.

A ring brooch used to close a garment at the neck is illustrated (48). It is set with rubies and sapphires and is engraved 'I am here in place of the friend I love'. Another

49 Every castle would have its
own chapel; the day began with mass
(*Book of Hours, Osterreichische
Nationalbibliothek, Vienna*)

48 Ring brooch,
13th century
(*British Museum*)

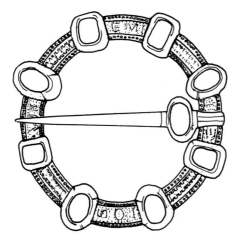

brooch of the same date found at Writtle in Essex had the inscription 'I am a brooch to guard the breast, that no rascal may put his hand thereon'.

She wore a mantle or cloak tied with cords across her chest or fastened with a brooch. The materials varied according to her means. If her husband had been to the Crusades she was probably lucky enough to have fine silks and muslins from the East, which lent themselves to more gathers and pleats than homespun wool or linen.

Velvet appeared from Italy in the 13th century and although styles changed little over several hundred years, variations were achieved by the use of different materials, a variety of furs which were extensively used on gowns, linings, collars, shoes and coats and which included rat and mole skins, and by embroidery on sleeves and hems and around necks. Girdles were of gold and silver cord for the wealthy and coloured wool, knotted at intervals, for the lesser ranks. Mantles, cloaks, and brooches were often given as presents, and so were gloves.

Changes in fashion did take place, especially in the clothes the ladies wore on state occasions. They added trains to their gowns; in different periods their sleeves ended in incredible widths at the wrists, eventually needing to be tied in knots to keep them from trailing on the ground. In the 12th century there was a fashion for hair to be plaited. It was grown very long and bound with ribbon-bands, the lengths of the plaits being increased by the addition of long metal cylinders. It is no wonder that the many treatises on manners advised ladies to walk with dignity, neither trotting or running.

For the most part hair was shown as little as possible and there were all kinds of head-dresses. The wimple was the most popular and lasted for 200 years, simple and white for the ordinary countrywoman and ornamented and with a fine veil hanging from it for the wealthy.

In its basic form the wimple consisted of a piece of linen pinned to the hair on either side of the face and draped round the neck and throat. A veil, if worn, passed over the wimple and was held in place by a small metal fillet or band.

By the 14th century only widows continued to wear this form of head-dress. By this time ladies were also experimenting with modest corsetting and garments were made to fit their figures more closely.

Life at the top

Starting the day with mass in the chapel (49) was part of the daily routine of almost everyone in the Middle Ages; only the humblest classes restricted their attendance to Sundays and feast days in the parish church. Every castle and many a lesser dwelling had its chapel and chaplain. The latter also acted as secretary and agent of the lord and as tutor to his children.

It was not considered right or necessary for a girl to learn to read unless she was to become a nun. One reason given was that she might read 'follies' written by men which they would not dare to speak or send by messenger. From the accounts of many formidable ladies of the time it seems that not many followed this advice. Convents taught many girls of high rank reading, writing and needlework.

Most civilizing influences came from the Church, from convents and from

monasteries, both in learning and in medicine. Hospitals were run by monks and nuns and since herbs were the foundation of most medication the monks pioneered herb gardens. Surgery was dangerous but sometimes a necessity. The gist of a 14th-century surgeon's advice was as follows: 'Drug and sandbag the patient unconscious, tie up securely; if you must cut, do so boldly; loss of blood is less, and shock minimized. If necessary bathe in warm water to restore temperature, put to bed, keep warm; feed well.'

As well as a chapel in the house or tower there was often a separate chapel in the bailey, of such importance that it was often the first building of the castle to be built in stone. An example is the tiny stone chapel built for Queen Margaret of Scotland at Edinburgh Castle. This Saxon princess was an exceptionally devout Christian, who before she died, under the age of fifty, had brought up eight children, done much to initiate reforms in Scotland, especially in the Church, and had earned the love and affection of all by her unceasing work for the poor and the example of her piety. She was an example of what was considered the high ideal for which a noble lady should aim. She was later canonized as a saint. Her small oratory, only 4 metres or so by 9 metres (roughly 14 feet by 32 feet) is the only building of this early date that has survived the long and stormy history of this castle.

In noble families breakfast after mass was at seven, and was probably only a light meal of bread and ale. The main meal was at ten or eleven in the morning, supper came at four in the afternoon, and light refreshments were eaten in the bedroom between eight and nine before retiring. This was to make the most of the daylight hours. Lighting by rushlights, or by candles for those who could afford them, was expensive and of poor quality.

Main meals were very formal and the most important books of the age apart from religious works were manuals of etiquette. The lord and his family and guests sat on three sides of the top table at one end of the hall on a raised dias. The rest of the company sat on benches at trestle tables down each side of the hall (51.1). Only the lord and perhaps his lady or important guests sat on chairs. This was the time of the day when those who wished to ask a special favour could approach the lord in supplication. Travellers were always welcomed at the table and the news they brought repaid the hospitality (51.2).

Table manners

The meal commenced with the washing of hands, considered essential in medieval times. Servants carried water in ewers or 'aquamaniles', which were often shaped like animals whose mouths formed the open tops. They poured the water over the diners' hands, catching it in a bowl underneath. The hands were then wiped on a towel which the servant carried over his arm. The ritual was repeated again at the end of the meal when hands were greasy after eating with the fingers.

Knives and spoons were used, but forks were at first unknown, and were still rare in the 14th century. The table was laid with a cloth and the food was served from dishes of glazed pottery, pewter and silver. Silver spoons, cups and platters were a mark of wealth. The salt cellar was a particularly important item, diners sitting above or 'below the salt' according to rank. Each diner brought his own knife to the table.

Meat was the principal item on the menu, cooked on a spit and served from it at the table (52). Pork and poultry figured largely in the diet, several birds being cooked on one spit. Both pigs and poultry were reared in large quantities as they could fend for themselves to a large extent. Beef cattle and sheep were small in comparison with today's animals and were kept principally for their skins, wool and dairy produce.

There was little fodder to keep any but breeding stock through the winter, so any surplus animals were slaughtered and the

51.1 Dinner time:
only the lord is seated
on a chair
(*British Museum*)

51.2 Women
making up a bed
for a traveller
(*British Museum*)

meat was salted or smoked for use in the winter months. The diet was supplemented with venison and game from the hunting of which the Normans were so fond. Hunting in his own forest was now strictly the lord's prerogative, and anyone poaching on his preserves risked death or maiming. While the lord and his guests ate the venison, the heart, liver and entrails known as 'umbles' were made into umble pie for lesser mortals.

The other source of meat in winter was the lord's dovecote and even when space was so precious many castles devoted part of one of the towers to housing pigeons. At Tattershall in Lincolnshire the whole south-west turret on the second floor was lined with a dovecote. The pigeons also provided eggs and fertilizer. When Richard II dined with his uncle John of Gaunt in 1387, 1,200 pigeons and 11,000 eggs were on the menu.

The other staple item of diet was of course bread. All corn had to be brought to the lord's mill to be ground, to which the growers deeply objected. No doubt many housewives illicitly ground their own corn, rye or beans on a quern as in Roman and Saxon times, baking it on a griddle over their fire.

Bread was not only eaten, but also cut into thick slices and used as plates or trenchers. Usually two people shared a place at table, men serving women. Those who were still hungry could end the meal by eating the plate, but there were plenty of dogs and probably many beggars as well waiting for any remains, as meals in the hall were rather public affairs even when the castle owner was the king. Although etiquette manuals advised against stroking cats and dogs at mealtimes, pets were popular and ladies did have lap dogs which they fed at the table.

Sweetmeats and dried and fresh fruit were eaten at the end of the meal. A great deal of wine was imported from France by the Normans, but ale, cider, perry and mead were also drunk, mostly by the lower orders. Wines medicated with herbs and spices were used for the treatment of various diseases. For example fennel wine was thought to relieve eye disorders, nausea and pleurisy.

Before the Crusaders brought back spices from the East together with a taste for food cooked with them, medieval food was not highly spiced. Many of the prepared dishes, apart from the food served at great feasts, were made from simple ingredients. There was mutton broth with onions and barley. Pottage was a term applied to the various mixtures of meat and vegetables, or in the case of poor people of vegetables alone, simmered over the fire in the cauldron.

53 The kitchen of
Berkeley Castle, 14th
century (*page 54*)
(*English Life
Publications Ltd*)

People also enjoyed bacon and beans, brawn, ham and eggs, omelettes with parsley and, on the very many fast days ordered by the Church, a great quantity of fish with a variety of sauces. Large quantities of mustard were used and a type of mint sauce was served with meat and bread sauce with poultry. There were baked apples and milk puddings; there were pears stewed in honey and a little vinegar and served with cream; there were oatcakes and gingerbread.

Cooking was still done in the open if possible or in a separate outdoor kitchen, if there was one, because of the danger of fire, and what is more it was done by men. The castle seems to have been the only type of home in history where the kitchen was not full of women. In fact the whole household was run by the steward who kept careful daily accounts, although the lady of the castle was quite able to supervise him whenever her husband was away.

The cooking was of necessity on a large scale and the utensils used were heavy. Eventually when kitchens were built inside castles they were built to a great height, the smoke and the intense heat escaping through a hole or louvre in the roof. The heat was so great that many of the cooks worked naked and can be seen in illustrations protecting themselves from the fire with what look like, and probably were, old archery targets used as fire-screens. The kitchen at Berkeley Castle is illustrated (53), showing the large assortment of spits available, and one of several fireplaces.

Kitchen equipment
The nearby buttery has sinks of solid lead, a large pestle and mortar for pounding food and herbs, a chopping block and the remains of earlier bread ovens. Most medieval recipes start with the instruction to 'smite him to pecys' so the chopping block was obviously well used.

Although kitchens were improved and acquired more equipment (54) during succeeding centuries they did not change a great deal, as the amount of food to be prepared was still great. The kitchen at St Fagans Castle near Cardiff (55) had a spit driven by a small dog walking round inside the circular cage. From the ceiling a large bread crate is suspended, one that could hold a complete baking of bread and keep it safe from rats and mice. There is also a bacon rack suspended from the ceiling to hang smoked and salted meat for use during the winter.

By the 13th and 14th centuries castle walls and gateways had been strengthened considerably. It was then considered safe for all the residential apartments to be moved down to ground level and increasingly, more attention was given to the comfort of the inhabitants. Windows could now be larger and were protected by shutters held in place by iron bars, and glass was increasingly used to let in more light and keep out the wind. Window seats were built in the walls beneath.

Behind a secure wall (sometimes two walls with defending towers as well), more and more buildings appeared in the grounds of existing castles. These provided extra living rooms for the family,

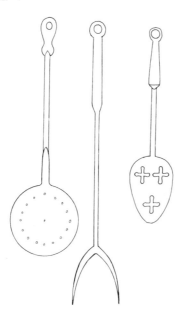

54 Early cooking utensils

welcome accommodation for guests and their retinues and space for the many activities connected with the running of the castle.

Bodiam Castle in Sussex, built at the end of the 14th century, was designed with its residential quarters conveniently arranged inside the walls in a quadrangle, instead of the previously haphazard development of isolated buildings in earlier castles. It contained numerous private chambers, with one set of rooms for the lord and his family and a completely separate set of rooms for his retainers, who had their own dining hall.

A great baron was far above a simple knight, and the early homes of these knights (and of many people of similar rank for centuries to come) were very small and simple by contrast with the quarters of their lord and lady. In the castle grounds at Christchurch in Dorset there are the remains of a house built in stone about 1106. It belonged to the warden or constable in charge of the castle.

There is only one big room, on the first floor above the ground-floor store room: the communal room where the knight, his family, his retainers and his dogs lived, ate and slept. It was 20 metres by 7 metres (about 67 feet by 23 feet) and had three windows on both of the long sides, each containing two openings with rounded arches. It had a large fireplace and a round chimney, unusual at this early date, one of the oldest chimneys now in existence.

There are doors to what must have been outbuildings and a kitchen, but there were no private quarters for the family and the only privacy at night would have been

55 The kitchen at St Fagans, Cardiff, 16th century, with furniture of the 17th and 18th centuries (*Welsh Folk Museum*)

56 Painted screen with
original decoration,
16th century, in the
hall of Berkeley Castle
(*English Life
Publications Ltd*)

provided by curtains or screens. Originally there was a garde-robe or lavatory in the thickness of the wall. In the 13th century a small two-storey block was built projecting over the stream which protected one wall, with a lavatory on the ground floor and a look-out tower above.

Where the domestic quarters of a castle could be expanded, a withdrawing room or solar was situated either above the hall or behind the high table where the lord and his family dined. At the other end of the hall there was a screen protecting the occupants from draughts from the entrance (56). Beyond the screen was a passage serving the kitchen, buttery and pantry, and above it was often a minstrels'

gallery where musicians played during meals. Music was considered soothing and beneficial by physicians and ladies learned to become very proficient on the harp and viol.

Apart from painted screens and woodwork all the castle would be decorated inside and out. The plain stone walls we see today were covered with whitewash or bright colours, painted designs on religious or moral themes and painted cloths and tapestries. Originally the White Tower at the Tower of London was actually painted white.

As in Anglo-Saxon times much of the colour, comfort and decoration in the castle was provided by the women, working away at their spinning and weaving, sewing and embroidery (57.2). Apart from clothes they made bedcovers, wall coverings, seat coverings, cushions, embroidered carpets for tables (rushes were used to cover floors) and vestments and cloths for use in the chapel.

The first spinning wheel

Spinning still depended mainly on the spindle and distaff, but the first spinning wheels were introduced in the 14th century. The early wheels were of the 'muckle wheel' type (57.1), where the wheel is hand turned. They were in use in the remoter areas of the British Isles until recent times and could be home-made without much difficulty. This must have been the kind on which the Sleeping Beauty pricked her finger before falling asleep for a hundred years in her castle, because the spindle consists of a thin rod of iron with a sharp point. The spindle is connected to the wheel with a band. As the wheel is turned the spinner steps backwards, drawing out and twisting the thread as she goes. When the wheel is reversed the spindle winds the wool she has spun. It has been estimated that a woman could walk 20 miles in a day's spinning. The ladies in their castle towers perhaps got more exercise than one might think. The muckle wheel was followed by the treadle wheel which has a bobbin that is automatically filled as the yarn is spun.

The influence of women on new decorations and improvements in a castle was considerable. Time and again we find that a room is redecorated for a marriage or a birth: new hangings are ordered for beds, new tapestries for walls. Henry III had glass put in his queen's chamber at Windsor on his marriage in 1236 to Eleanor of Provence. The windows overlooked a garden, not so unusual a feature of a castle as one might imagine. Fish ponds, orchards and vineyards are also found near castle walls. When the queen gave birth to the future Edward I three years later a nursery was provided for him,

57.1 Muckle wheel (*National Museum of Antiquities, Scotland*)

57.2 The furnishings of the castle were provided by the women (*British Museum*)

wainscotted and with iron bars at the windows, though these were probably intended to keep intruders out rather than to keep the child in.

Mary Queen of Scots was no stranger to castles, and spent many long hours at her embroidery during her later imprisonment. She moved into Edinburgh Castle in June 1566 to await the birth of her son James, who was to become James VI of Scotland and later James I of England. The midwife who attended her was given a special black velvet dress for the event and the Queen's bed had new hangings of blue taffeta and blue velvet. The baby's cot was covered with yards of Holland cloth.

The birth was a long and difficult one, despite the efforts of the Countess of Atholl to transfer the pain by means of witchcraft from the Queen to Lady Reres.

Although employing a wet-nurse as was the custom of the time, Mary did have the baby to sleep in her own room, watching over him at night and devoting her time to caring for him for the month she was at Edinburgh. She later arranged for her son to be transferred to Stirling Castle where he was to be brought up by the Erskine family. Mary ordered gold and silver buckets for the nursery at Stirling, blue plaiding for the baby's cradle and plaiding and a canopy for Lady Reres' bed, as well as blankets and feather bolsters. The walls were to be hung with tapestries. An embroidered wall covering of this date from Berkeley Castle is illustrated (58).

Fostering the children

Most noblewomen in the Middle Ages handed over their sons, and sometimes their daughters as well, to others to be brought up, taking into their own homes the children of other families to act as pages and ladies in waiting. The fostering of children was eventually copied in homes further down the social scale. Children were betrothed when only a few years old, and many girls married at 14. Childhood was short.

Castles that were in continuous occupation through the centuries do seem to have kept pace with all the changes in furnishings and arrangement of rooms that went on in what we think of as more

58 Embroidered wall covering, 16th century, Berkeley Castle (*English Life Publications Ltd*)

59 Elizabeth Drax:
Sir Joshua Reynolds;
Berkeley Castle, 18th
century (*page 61*)
(*English Life
Publications Ltd*)

domestic buildings. Elizabethan ladies liked a long gallery to walk in on winter days and in which the children could play, and at Powis Castle in Wales, still occupied today, a magnificent long gallery, noted for the quality of its plaster work, was built at the end of the 16th century. A grand staircase was a 17th-century addition; no more perilous climbing up and down twisting stairs. Windows were enlarged and walls wainscotted.

Gradually castles acquired fine furni-ture, carpets and paintings. When the Roundheads seized Corfe Castle in Dorset in 1646, they took away a large quantity of tapestries, damask hangings, satin cush-ions, Turkey and Persian carpets, ebony cabinets, beds with luxurious furnishings, trunks of fine clothes and books. The castle had been defended for 48 days by Lady Mary Banks with 80 soldiers, before she surrendered.

On many occasions when a castle owner was away the women seem to have taken

60 Medieval
woman painter; detail
from a manuscript
(*British Museum*)

over the defence of the building with great efficiency. Lady Banks, her daughters and her women took their part in heaving down stones and hot embers to prevent the enemy scaling the castle walls.

Not all castle ladies needed to be so active. Embroidery was still the occupation of many ladies in the 18th century. In the long drawing room at Berkeley Castle there is a complete suite of gilt furniture, settee, chairs and stools (one of the stools is dated 1749), embroidered in petit-point by Elizabeth Drax, the wife of the fourth Earl (59).

We must not however get the impression that the women of the castle in earlier centuries were shut up for years on end spinning and sewing. Owners of great estates were forever on the move from one of their castles to another or to a manor or hunting lodge, which involved packing on a grand scale. This is why furniture and hangings were movable and chests are the largest items of furniture remaining from the Middle Ages. Everything that was movable was moved, packed on horses and carts and taken to the next castle or manor where the whole retinue stayed, probably until the food there had run out, when they moved on again.

Early beds could be dismantled and only when beds, tables and chairs became too ornate and heavy to move did they remain behind. Valuables were locked in sturdy chests bound with iron bars and a lady probably took her jewellery in a small casket decorated with ivory or enamel. Travel on horseback for many miles was usual for all. A lady could travel in a long covered wagon if she chose, in more elegance but less comfort.

She also accompanied her husband on pilgrimages and to tournaments. When not actually fighting or preparing to fight, keeping in practice by fighting at tournaments was a popular occupation for noblemen and knights.

Special stands were erected for the ladies at these events, and not always well erected. Queen Philippa and her ladies fell unhurt from a collapsing stand in the 14th century and the carpenters who erected it were only saved from punishment by the Queen appealing to her husband on her knees.

Hawking was another activity in which women could join their husbands. Women were considered especially good in training the young birds, and many ladies would have perches in their rooms for their falcons. Some also went hunting, especially for foxes, badgers and other small game. Life was lived to a large extent out of doors in medieval times, but the shortage of space and furnishings indoors must have been oppressive during the long, dark winters, especially for the women and children. It is not surprising that spring was greeted with such enthusiasm by medieval people and poets alike – an enthusiasm that found expression in songs in praise of May day.

The Manor House

The lady of the manor was a hard-working housewife . . . most of the necessities of life were supplied from the estate and prepared in the brewhouse, bakehouse, dairy and kitchen

The 15th century chapel of Cotehele House in the west country (*page 66*) (*The National Trust, L. Gayton*)

In the 14th and 15th centuries many manor houses were little more than the simple one-roomed hall of the Anglo-Saxons. They were only slowly provided with private quarters for the lord and lady and domestic quarters for the retinue. There was still a central fire, and only gradually were chimneys built on outside walls to take away the smoke from wall fireplaces.

The manor was still surrounded by a moat, for if the king of the time was weak, as in the 15th century, the home still had to be defended, and the lord of the manor was not always around to help his wife. She had to be prepared to cope when he was at war, in court in London defending his right to his land, or even possibly in prison if he had been unsuccessful in any of these exploits.

As the manor was to some extent a self-supporting unit, all food, clothes and furnishings had to be provided for many months ahead for the whole household and the lady of the manor was responsible for seeing that this was done. Life may have been continually busy, often dangerous, but it can never have been dull.

Many of these small manor houses have been adapted as peaceful comfortable homes for modern living, and it is difficult now to imagine the fear and panic, intrigue and despair that filled their walls on so many occasions in the past.

What life was like for the women while their husbands were away can be learned from the letters of Margaret Paston, written to her husband John in London in the 15th century. She looked after Caister Castle and its estates in Norfolk with, apparently, little difficulty, making crucial decisions without consulting her husband. She obviously had a detailed knowledge of the day-to-day business of dealing with tenants, who were by this time paying rents in lieu of the feudal duties they had performed in Norman times, and much accounting work must have been involved.

While her husband was away in 1449, Margaret Paston, with only twelve men to help her, tried to defend their manor house against a force of 1,000 men sent by a rival claimant to drive her out. This they did by mining the walls of the chamber she was in and cutting the posts of the house so that it fell down. It needed petitions to Parliament and the Lord Chancellor before the Pastons regained possession.

The Pastons are typical of the many up-and-coming landowners of the time. They rose to power during the 14th century by acquiring manor after manor through inheritance or marriage and by placing their children to be brought up in the houses of greater landowners, from whom they hoped to receive favours and support.

Land was wealth, the only real wealth of the time, and families like the Pastons spent much of the time fighting each other for the ownership of land, both physically and in the courts of law. Between the nobility these contests for power became full-scale battles during the Wars of the Roses in the second half of the century.

Marrying for gain

The Paston family and the newcomers among the gentry had to become skilled lawyers to hang on to what they had acquired. It is clear that the Paston ladies were as conversant with the law and as well able to deal with their enemies as were their men.

Their marriages had been arranged by their parents when they were quite young and were largely contracts to increase their families' wealth and position and to obtain the best possible terms for both parties. No one was bothered by this and the lack of pre-marital romance does not seem to have prevented the marriages from becoming real partnerships in affection, respect and the pursuit of mutual aims.

The lady of the manor was a hard-working housewife. If she had sufficient servants she would not have to deal with the cleaning and the preparation of meals, but she was responsible for ordering food and clothing for the whole household and for making sure that supplies did not run

out, particularly during the long, difficult medieval winter. Most of the necessities of life were supplied from the estate and prepared in the brewhouse, bakehouse, dairy and kitchen.

The constable's house at Christchurch, Dorset, described on page 56, was an example of the plan of the earliest type of manor house. Eventually, when it was considered safe enough, the main hall was built on the ground floor instead of above it, and two-storey wings were added at one or both ends. The lady of the manor had her solar or private living room on the first floor, with a squint-hole in the wall so that she could see what was happening in the hall below. At Cotehele in Cornwall there is one squint-hole to the hall and one on the other side of the solar to the chapel.

A chapel was usual in most manor houses of any size. The resident priest exercised a great influence on the family, acting as secretary, companion, adviser and agent to the lord and his lady. The position and influence of the chaplain to Margaret Paston after her husband died was greatly resented by her children.

The hall was made a little less draughty by the screens passage, and a porch was added to give further protection. Compton Wynyates in Warwickshire, built between 1480 and 1520, was one of the first Tudor houses to have a porch.

The windows were covered with panes of horn or linen dipped in wax. The first window to have glass (often stained glass)

was the large oriel window at the end of the hall where the lord sat, looking towards the entrance gate, so that he could see who was approaching his home. The large oriel windows became the bay windows of the later homes. Great Chalfield manor in Wiltshire, built at the end of the 15th century, is a good example of the later development of the manor house. It is built around a courtyard at the back of the hall, giving extra living accommodation, kitchen quarters and stables.

Where the fire in the hall was still in the centre of the room, as it was in many halls well into Elizabethan times, the smoke no longer drifted out through an open hole in the roof. Elaborate coverings or louvres of horizontal slats of wood set diagonally covered the hole, letting out smoke and keeping out rain.

The floors were of stone, hard-beaten chalk, or earth covered with rushes. Some tiled floors appeared in the reign of Henry III, a fashion brought to England by his French wife. Carpets were used, but still only for covering tables and not floors. Furniture was still sparse and the chest continued to be the all-purpose piece of the time, used for storage, as a bed and as a seat.

Tapestry cut like wallpaper

The walls were covered extensively by tapestries or painted cloths, giving colour and warmth, and it is interesting to see at Cotehele that they were used much as we use wallpaper, cut to fit round corners and doorways regardless of the pictures on them.

Most of the money spent in the home went on furnishings and not furniture. Hangings kept out draughts round the four-poster beds and were considered more important than the woodwork. There might have been a livery cupboard with ventilation holes in it in the bedroom to hold late-night snacks of bread or wine; liveries were the rations given to the household for late meals.

When Renaissance ideas of decoration

66 Bread baking in a brick wall oven with an iron door (*Welsh Folk Museum*)

penetrated to the country homes of England they were added to the Gothic buildings, in a way never seen on the continent, as and where the occupants felt inclined. The lady of the manor probably found an elaborate plaster ceiling added to her Gothic-windowed solar, with linenfold panelling on her walls.

The kitchen at Cotehele was completed by 1520. It leads from the hall of the same date but as so often happened when improvements were made, later dining rooms at Cotehele moved further and further away from the kitchen. Hot meals and convenience were gradually sacrificed to privacy.

The Cotehele kitchen (65) is not large but it is very high, as all medieval kitchens had to be to dissipate the smoke and heat from the 3 metre (roughly 10 feet) wide hearth and the 2 metre (7 feet) wide oven at the other end of the kitchen. This oven would have been used for baking bread, pies and cakes and was heated, as all such ovens were until recent times, by building a fire of sticks or furze inside it until the walls were hot. The ashes were then raked out and the food to be baked was put inside with the help of a long-handled wooden oven peel (67.1).

Baking in a brick oven continued in farmhouses and cottages from the Middle

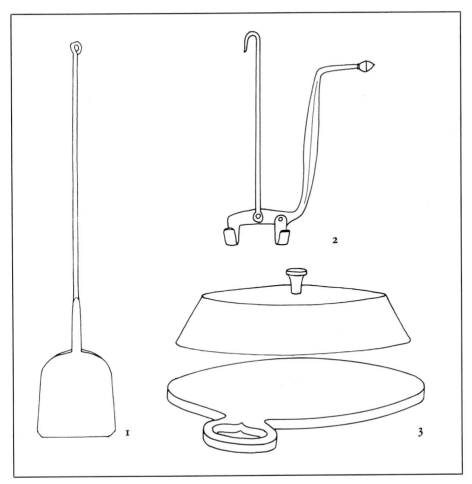

67.1 Oven peel

67.2 Kettle tilter
(*page 68*)

67.3 Bake iron
(19th century)
(*page 68*)

Ages until very recent times (66). Bread could also be baked on the floor of the hearth under a bake-iron (67.3), which had hot ashes packed all over it, and this method was used in small farmhouses and cottages where there was no bread oven.

Pure wheat bread, known as manchet, was eaten only by the wealthy or on great occasions. The most common bread eaten was made of rye, or rye and wheat mixed. In some households pea and bean meal was mixed in and others used barley. When the harvest was poor, everyone had to use substitutes, and peas and beans were common crops grown by all to dry and store for winter use.

The flour was milled at the manor mill, which at Cotehele is half a mile from the house and which has been restored to working order by the National Trust. There is also a horse-powered cider mill nearby, a blacksmith's forge, a wheelwright's shop and a sawpit where the trees from the manor woodland were sawn into planks, for use on the estate and for making some of the furniture in the house. Furniture was all made to order by estate and village carpenters at this date.

The amount of timber used during the Middle Ages in building castles and houses as well as for fuel was tremendous. Oak beams 30 centimetres (a foot) or more square are everywhere. To obtain a beam of this size and 7.5 metres (about 25 feet) in length an oak tree some 300 years old would need to be cut down. It is not surprising that by the end of the Elizabethan period a wood shortage was becoming apparent and coal was being increasingly used as fuel. This speeded up the building of chimneys. Wood smoke was bearable in a central fire, but coal smoke was not.

In the photograph of Cotehele kitchen (65) pot hooks with adjustable hangers to take kettles and cauldrons can be seen hanging in the hearth. The kettle has a 'handy-maid' device (67.2), which can tip a kettle or pot forward and reduce the effort of lifting heavy utensils when pouring liquids. In place of the modern thermostat there are hooks at various heights to control the heat under the cauldron by lifting or lowering it.

Cooking in a Cauldron

In place of 'constant hot water' the hot-water cauldron on the left of the picture has a tap to facilitate drawing off water as needed. There is a chimney crane (69.1) to position the pots over the fire and swing them clear when the food is cooked. This again is adjustable vertically as well as horizontally. All these improvements suggest that women were in this kitchen supervising the meals and that as time passed they had ordered or talked the estate blacksmith into making life a little easier for them.

The kitchen has a giant-sized pestle and mortar and large chopping block, because it was still necessary for the cook to do a lot of 'smiting him to pecys'. Pounded meat was mixed with yolk of egg and spices and cooked, probably in a bag, in a cauldron. Pounded meat was also mixed with raisins, almonds, cinnamon and sugar, onions, cloves, ginger and rice.

It is likely that except on feast days the cauldron was in use more than the spit as there were many soups, pottages and stews eaten with spoons. Several dishes could be cooked at the same time in one cauldron, as is done in a modern pressure cooker.

The picture shows the unique racked dogs at Cotehele which could hold spits of various kinds at a variety of heights and could be taken out of the hearth when not in use. The spit on the shelf at the side in the illustration is a basket type (69.2) which could hold a large fish or a sucking pig without its having to be pierced.

Iron fire-dogs kept the logs in place and got their name from their shape in silhouette. One type had holders at the top where hot drinks could be placed to keep warm (69.3).

A long dripping pan below the spit caught the fat from the roasting meat. There were very thin spits on which

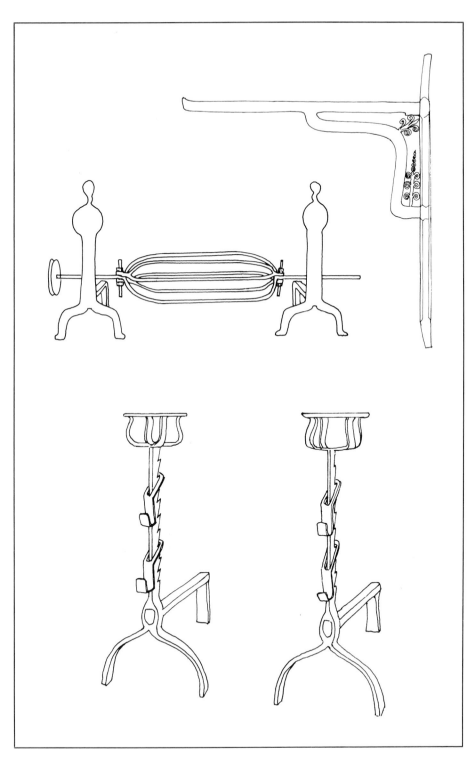

69.1 Chimney crane
(*Welsh Folk Museum*)

69.2 Basket spit

69.3 Wrought iron
cup-dogs

70.1 Cornish trivets or brandises (*North Cornwall Museum*)

70.2 Salt box

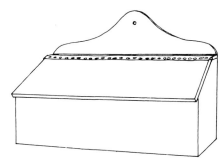

70.3 Grease pan (*page 72*)

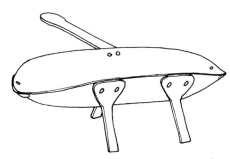

several of the small birds popular at the time, such as larks and thrushes, could be cooked. Food could be kept warm on a variety of brandises, the west-country name for trivets (70.1). These were designed not to tip over and could also stand in the embers with a pot on them for further cooking.

Food that needed additional browning after baking received the attentions of a salamander; this was a long-handled iron implement with a flat end which was made red-hot in the fire and held over the pies and cakes. Most of the utensils had exceptionally long handles to protect the cooks from the heat of the fire.

The shelves at the side of the kitchen hold the pewter ware and cloam ware now relegated to the kitchen though good enough for the hall in the 14th and 15th centuries. Wooden trenchers were eventually slipped under the bread trenchers and were square like the bread they replaced. Often they were carved with a small indentation for salt in the corner.

Salting away for the winter

Salt was a most important item in medieval life, principally as the means of preserving meat, bacon and fish for the winter months. Margaret Paston bought herrings by the barrel for this purpose.

Salt for daily use was kept as near to the fire as possible to keep it dry, either in a small recess in the brickwork of the fireplace or in a wooden box (70.2), with leather hinges to prevent corrosion, hanging at the side. In Scotland, where wood was in short supply, the salt was kept in a 'saat cuddie', 60 centimetres (2 feet) high, a straw bag with a square hole in the middle.

Meat was also preserved by smoking, outdoors at first and later in the large chimneys over wood fires. Oak sawdust from the sawpit was a popular fuel for smoking, but more popular still was the rough outside part of oak bark. The inner oak bark was used by the tanner for tanning leather. The outside 'sole' was put aside for bacon curing.

There must have been some very good smells floating around the kitchen court at Cotehele, from the smoking meat, the roasting meat and the bread and pies in the bread oven, to say nothing of the smell of ale brewing in the brewing coppers, although it seems unlikely that anything was needed to tempt medieval appetites.

One of the main requisites of any home after food and warmth was light, and for centuries this was provided by candle and rushlights. Cressets, early medieval lamps made of stone or iron were also used. In these lighted wicks floated in a pool of oil. Those who could afford them bought town-made candles from the wax-chandler or from itinerant salesmen. These were made of wax or tallow and were placed in wooden, silver or pewter candlesticks sometimes 3 metres (10 feet) high holding several candles. There were also hanging candelabra of brass, wood or iron, suspended from the ceiling by pulleys, ropes and chains.

Candles were an expensive item and even if they owned several manors and much land, the lords of the manor were usually short of ready cash for purchasing goods in shops or markets, so economy in household items was necessary and as much as possible would be home-made. Margaret Paston had to write to her husband in London on one occasion to warn him that she was down to her last four shillings and would have to borrow money unless he came home soon.

In poorer homes people made their own candles and rushlights from kitchen fat. Mutton fat was preferred as it was the hardest. These burned and spluttered like a torch, or flickered faintly when the tallow grew thin. They continued to be the main source of light in many country homes until the last century.

The thin rushes were gathered by women and children in midsummer from the edges of streams and stripped of their green surface till only the soft white pith was left, supported by one thin remaining strip of the green rind to hold it together

71.1 Rushlight made from peeled rushes dipped in fat melted in a holder; the small brush is made from the peel of the rushes (*Welsh Folk Museum*)

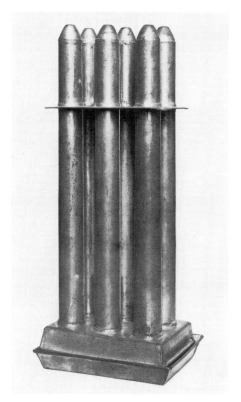

71.2 Candle mould (*Welsh Folk Museum*)

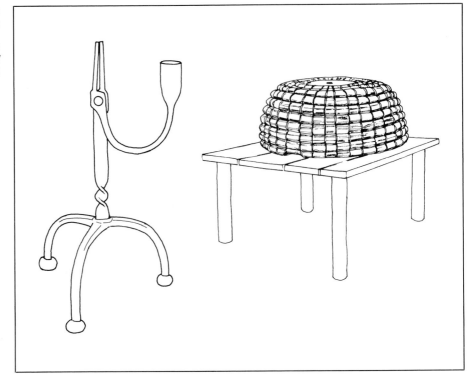

along its length. This served as a wick. The fat was then melted over a fire in a grease pan (70.3) or candle-dipper, and the wicks were laid in it until the fat soaked into them. They were then taken out, cooled and dipped again and again until the coating was thick enough, then laid on a piece of hollow bark to dry.

Such a taper would not fit the socket of the candlestick and was clasped in the scissor-like jaws of the rushlight holder. An early form of rushlight holder is illustrated (71.1), giving an idea of the small amount of light it provided. The rind stripped from the green rush has been made into a small brush, in true country fashion where nothing is wasted. In later examples there was a small candle socket on the movable end of the holder to take home-made candles (72.1). These were made at first by dipping the rushes continually until a thicker coating of tallow was obtained. Later cotton wicks were

used and the fat poured into candle moulds (71.2). There were also rushlight holders on stands. A rushlight some 30 to 40 centimetres (12 to 15 inches) long would burn for about half an hour. It had to receive constant attention, being pushed upwards every five minutes, a job that was probably given to children when their mother was busy.

Weaving and spinning were still done at home, but by the 15th century in several towns clothiers provided the raw materials for cottage workers in surrounding villages to spin and weave, collecting the finished cloth which could then be bought in the town. This still had to be made up into garments at home, for ready-made clothes were rare.

Margaret Paston was one of many wives who frequently asked any male relative going to London to bring back material. Hats, girdles and laces could also be bought in town and there were also repeated requests from medieval wives for spices, especially pepper, cloves, mace, ginger and cinnamon, and also for almonds, rice and raisins. They kept these spices in special boxes under lock and key.

Sugar loaves in blocks weighing about 4.5 kilogrammes (10 pounds) were now available, but most of the sweetening of food was still done with honey, and straw beehives (72.2) were important to manor, farm and cottage for many years to come.

Oranges and dates were obtainable in towns and one request for oranges by a medieval wife who longed for them is accompanied by apologies for having this longing although she was not pregnant.

The Paston family letters are full of requests for treacle from London, often it seems needed in a hurry for medicinal purposes.

Meeting the right people

The Paston letters are not all business and requests for goods. Time and again great concern is shown for the husband's health and safety, usually manifested in the most practical manner known to the ladies of the family by their going on a pilgrimage to some local shrine to pray for his recovery or safety. Chaucer's pilgrims were no literary make-believe; all kinds of people joined in this popular medieval pursuit. One of the Paston agents reported that when he went to collect the rents in one village, he came away empty-handed because almost the whole village had gone

on a pilgrimage to Canterbury. Religion was a major influence in everyone's lives and coloured their outlook on all they did.

The harsh conditions of life forced medieval people to be intensely practical both in their marriages and in their attitude to their children. They did their best to place their children at an early age in the household of someone higher up the social scale, where they could make the right contacts and, especially in the case of a girl, eventually make a suitable marriage.

The Paston family spent 10 years trying to arrange a marriage for John Paston's sister Elizabeth, regardless of the age or appearance of the men. She was kept housebound by her mother so that she could not get entangled with unsuitable men and only eventually agreed to marry one suitor after her mother had taken very strong measures. A relation wrote, 'She has since Easter (3 months ago) for the most part been beaten once in the week or twice, sometimes twice a day, and her head broken in two or three places.' In spite of this she seems to have ended her days as a dutiful, diligent housewife. As Dame Elizabeth Browne she left in her will fine home-made sheets, tablecloths, napkins and towels and seven feather beds.

Probably those further down the social scale and even the younger members of a large aristocratic family managed to marry for love, but it is difficult to find much evidence for the romantic knights of the Middle Ages outside literature.

The Elizabethan Farmhouse

Laundry was a sociable occasion, much of it taking place out of doors on a fine day and in the river if there was one nearby

Elizabethan housewives doing their washing in the open air *(page 82)* *(British Museum)*

For the 16th century housewife, awakening before dawn in her Elizabethan farmhouse, the outlook was brighter than it had been for 1300 years. There was hope, energy and vitality abroad in the land; more security, more prosperity, and the yeoman farmers of the country were enjoying the boom years along with the merchants and traders. It was possible for these farmers to rise under the Tudors to the highest positions in the land. William Cecil, Elizabeth's greatest counsellor, was of yeoman stock. It was the golden age of private enterprise.

The farmer might have built his wife a brand-new home by this time: timber-framed, with either wattle-and-daub or brick walls, or one of stone, according to the area in which they lived. (Local materials were always used in the building of 16th century homes, which is why they fit so well into the surrounding landscape.) At the very least he was sure to have made improvements to their existing farmhouse, giving her more comfort and privacy. The kitchen was more likely to be built in now, instead of being merely an outside shack.

There would be extra rooms for living and sleeping, and she might expect to look out on this brighter world through glass in her windows. Of course, not all change is easily accepted or afforded, and farmhouses were still being built at the end of the 16th century with windows which had only wooden bars and shutters.

Rooms were now more likely to have fireplaces; chimney pots were appearing on many roofs in a variety of designs. The ingle-nook fireplace was large enough to take built-in seats on each side, even if these were simply whole tree trunks built into the walls, and it made a warm sheltered spot, particularly for the old people. When the medieval chest grew a back and became a settle, the warm area was further enlarged by a settle on each side and often a curtain was drawn across as well to completely enclose the occupants.

In the 17th century farmhouse of Ken-nixton at St Fagans, Cardiff (77), there is a settle on one side of the fireplace and a box bedstead on the other side, of a type also well known in Scotland, showing that from the 16th century onwards at least, comfort and warmth for farmhouse inhabitants were becoming more and more in demand. These box bedsteads often had a shelf inside for a baby.

The fashion for 'separates'

It is to be hoped that the housewife now dressed in the morning in a warmer and less smoky atmosphere than her predecessors. The clothes she put on would depend to a large extent both on her status and on the weather. The Elizabethans were very fond of 'separates': even sleeves were separate items of clothing.

The number of kirtles and bodices, gowns and overgowns a woman wore would depend on how wealthy her husband was and how much time she had for dressing. Rich wives put on a type of housecoat on rising and took a great deal of time over dressing, but the farmer's wife probably wore a simple bodice with a small ruff at the neck and a long skirt of homespun cloth over her petticoat.

The more prosperous her husband became the larger grew her skirts, sleeves and ruffs, until it was obvious to the outside world that active housewifery in such an outfit was out of the question. It was the ambition and achievement of many yeoman farmers' wives and merchants' wives to become 'gentry'. Never was there such a movement up the social scale again until the 19th century.

If she had a mirror, it would be of polished metal. She wore a small linen cap at all times, even under her hat when she went out, and although most women kept their hair entirely hidden (as they had for centuries), a few now allowed a little hair to escape from under the cap. Washing was minimal, and only a small basin was used.

Many girls wore no shoes inside the farmhouse, or only thin slippers. They wore pattens (79.1) to raise them above the

mud outside and the ashes around the fire while cooking. These were in general use until the middle of the 19th century and were wooden clogs with a leather toe-piece and bands of leather that tied with a short lace over the instep. The oval iron hoop underneath lifted the wearer out of the mud. Without pattens a girl would be 'slip-shod'.

A large, long apron was worn by most Elizabethan women because almost all of them were in fact working housewives and a very large percentage were also country housewives. While the better off had more servants, and menservants to do the heavier work, all women, wealthy or not, closely supervised all the domestic activities in their homes, and it was still necessary to make sure that every household, large or small, had enough provisions to see them through the long winters.

Although glass in the windows must have made homes lighter, it was still necessary to make the most of the daylight hours. Thomas Tusser, who wrote a household manual for those Elizabethan housewives who could read, and who had time to do so, stressed that they themselves must be up and doing before 5 a.m. to set a good example to their maids.

Waking the servants was an easy task as all bedrooms were intercommunicating. Corridors were unusual until later in the century. The farmer and his wife would sleep in the middle room, usually at the top of the stairs, with maids and daughters on one side and sons and manservants on the other.

Stairs were probably little more than ladders in the 16th century. If there were only two upper rooms the men would sleep down in the hall as in medieval times. Many smaller farmhouses still had the one hall for everyone to eat and sleep in, with perhaps a parlour at one end. This parlour was a multi-purpose room, used both as a best living room and as the parents' bedroom.

Farmhouses needed to be large because families were large, and servants and family were all housed under one roof. One of the benefits of building a chimney stack into a house was that the fire no longer burned in the middle of the hall and so an upper floor could be constructed. In some cases the whole upper floor was boarded in; in others the hall was left open to the roof in the middle and upper rooms were created over the parlour at one end and the kitchen at the other, as was done in the 16th and 17th century alterations to Bayleaf farmhouse, now reconstructed at the Weald and Downland Open Air Museum at Singleton in Sussex.

The upper room was still called the solar or 'soller'. It was now no longer a private room for the master and lady of the house, but seems also to have been used as a store for apples, corn, wool or cheese; not so surprising when we think what we put in the 'spare room' of our homes today.

Furniture built to last
As rooms and possessions increased so did furniture. It reflected the general wealth and security by becoming almost immovable, very heavy and ornate. The dining table changed from the movable trestle type to the 'table dormant': – a table with fixed legs which stood in the middle of the room, with seating round it. In place of the old stools and benches, chairs gradually appeared round the dining table,

like stools with a back added (back-stools, in fact). Comfort, although still somewhat rigid, had entered the housewife's world.

It was obviously the great fear of a farmer who had provisioned his home with window glass, floorboards, painted cloths on the walls, panelling, settles, dormant tables, chairs and benches that these would be stripped out of the house on his death. Many wills stipulated that such things should remain in the house forever, the stipulation also extending to such unlikely things as locks, keys, gutters, doors and – unbelievably – ceilings. More often than not all these were to be left in place at least during the lifetime of the widow. It must have been a comfort to her to know that the newly acquired ceilings and windows were not to be pulled down around her when her husband died.

Great concern for their wives and children after their death is shown by Elizabethan husbands in their wills. The property usually went to the eldest son, but time and again he is directed to provide fuel, a place at the fireside, a certain room or rooms, food and care for his mother during her lifetime. Most farmers tried also to provide dowries for their daughters on marriage and a few pounds for their younger sons on their coming of age. Apart from this, money did not play a large part in country life. Everyone thought in terms of barter rather than cash.

The Elizabethans rejoiced in showing off their new prosperity, and carving which had earlier adorned churches was now applied to furniture. Storage units were increasingly needed by a housewife to house and display her new possessions. She wanted the world to see her wealth, and the court cupboard became one of the most popular articles for the display of silver, if she was rich enough, or more likely of pewter, which was increasingly taking the place of wooden utensils at the table. Many drinking vessels, buckets and pitchers on the farm were stave-built of oak, like a barrel, held together on the

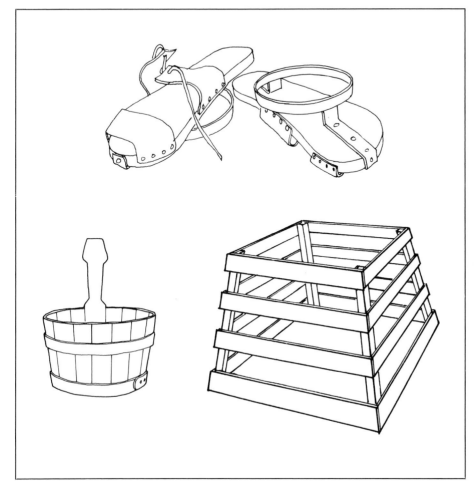

79.1 Pattens: a very practical form of footwear (*page 76*)

79.2 Staved drinking vessel 13 cm (5 in) in diameter

79.3 Baby walker, a cage-like device to safeguard a small child while his mother was busy, 16th century (*page 82*)

outside by binding laths of wood. One stave of the drinking vessels was lengthened to form a handle (79.2).

It is unlikely that a farmer's wife had any room completely furnished in the new Elizabethan style as museum reconstructions would suggest. Furniture was handed down from generation to generation and only replaced when worn out, so new items of furniture would only be added to a room as and when money was available.

The chest that had served the housewife well for centuries in which to store her few possessions was no longer adequate. Finding something at the bottom of a large chest was more difficult now that there was so much in it, and by the end of the 16th century drawers appeared at the bottom of the chest to ease this problem. This hybrid piece of furniture, a chest-on-drawers, is known as a mule chest.

Breakfast was only a snack: a dish of pottage, a little bread and meat. The morning would be a busy one, principally concerned with the preparation of the main meal, which was eaten at mid-day. The Elizabethans loved their food. It was considered necessary for good health, so the kitchen was an important part of the larger farm, coming in from the cold to be a carefully designed part of the farmhouse.

In smaller farmhouses the cooking would still be done in the fireplace in the hall, but where there was a separate kitchen it was much like the kitchen of the manor house, though perhaps on a smaller scale. The cooking utensils had increased from year to year, not so much in variety as in number, perhaps owing to the care with which they were handed on by women in their wills. They were often repaired but always cherished.

Large farmhouses had additional bake-houses, larders, pantries, a buttery and a dairy as in the manor house. These additional rooms were needed, for the kitchen quarters were a factory where many of the things a modern house-wife buys from a shop had to be made. Among the outbuildings at the farm at Wilmcote, near Stratford-on-Avon where Shakespeare's mother, Mary Arden, grew up, are a dovecote with 657 nesting-holes built inside its walls, and a cider mill. In a good apple year most farms of any size reckoned to make about 700 to 1,000 gallons of cider. They also brewed a constant supply of ale.

Animals were still slaughtered in the autumn, and all the meat had to be salted or smoked to preserve it. The English were already noted in the 16th century for the large quantities of meat they ate. When 'fish days' were no longer compulsory for religious reasons they were made compulsory to aid and protect the fishing industry, always one of the chief sources of men and ships for the Navy when needed. Practicality was a great Elizabethan virtue.

Venison pasties were popular and not found in any other country. Keeping meat fresh was a constant and not always successful task, and spices were used to mask the taste of tainted meat. One suggested method of restoring tainted venison was to wrap it in an old coarse cloth, and bury it in a hole in the ground to the depth of a metre (about 3 feet) for 12 to 20 hours. There were also many sauces to overcome the taste of bad meat, made in saucepans of silver, because of the danger of the action of vinegar and other acids upon copper vessels. These were served in 'sausers' – small rimless silver dishes, or if silver was out of the question, glass or earthenware was used.

Work in the dairy seems always to have been classed as women's work, and must have occupied a large part of their day. Only cheese, salted butter and bacon could be kept in store for long and these items were often left in his will to his widow by a farmer who wished to provide a supply of food and drink for her. Corn and malt for brewing ale were other items bequeathed.

Primrose pudding

Vegetables were eaten at the main meal, but many of the plants grown in Elizabethan kitchen gardens we would now class as flowers. Violets were chopped up with onions and lettuce for salad, or cooked with fennel and savory for broth. Stewed roses and primroses made the sort of choice dessert a hostess would boast about.

By the middle of the 16th century England was enjoying apricots, and cultivating strawberries, raspberries, gooseberries and melons. Improved varieties of strawberries were gradually produced but they were still only as large as blackberries. Rhubarb was used only as a drug, but saffron cakes were famous and saffron was also used to colour 'Warden' pies, the name given to pies made with Warden pears. New vegetables were introduced such as asparagus, artichokes, horseradish and eventually the potato.

Only labourers' wives were expected to work in the fields. The yeoman's wife worked in the garden, kitchen and dairy and perhaps looked after poultry, in much the same way as her modern counterpart.

The extra ornamentation in Elizabethan homes gradually extended outside to the elaborate knot garden. This often repeated some architectural detail of the house, with low clipped box, juniper, yew or lavender hedges outlining the complicated patterns of the flower beds. In winter, when there were no flowers, the pattern of the hedges still added interest to the garden. The raised beds contained cornflowers, cowslips, daffodils, daisies, hollyhocks, irises, lilies, marigolds, mint, pansies, paeonies, periwinkles, poppies, primroses, snapdragons, stocks, sweet marjoram, sweet william, wallflowers and violets.

Growing her own medicines

The great interest of the English in gardens developed during the 16th century, the owners of wealthier homes searching far afield for unusual plants for their gardens. Sir Walter Raleigh not only introduced tobacco to this country but imported many foreign seeds and plants for the first time. To meet the increasing interest in the subject the first gardening books were published.

Thomas Tusser, who was prolific in handing out advice to the housewives of the time, had no time for importing plants and seeds from abroad. In his book *The Points of Huswifery united to the comfort of Husbandry* he said it was the housewife's duty to collect her own seeds and to exchange plants with her neighbours, a practice that has been going on both before and since his time. He added instructions on digging, sowing seeds and weeding, obviously of great importance, as a Lincolnshire gentleman writing in 1577 said that a good way to judge a wife was by the state of her garden.

The preparation of all medicaments and toilet necessities from herbs from her own garden was a priority. Professional medical help was scarce and all women were expected to deal with most injuries and illnesses in their families and among their servants. The herb garden was the most important part of the garden. It was not a hobby or leisure pursuit but a matter of life and death. Every part of the body was connected with certain herbs that were thought to benefit it. For instance, aniseed, eyebright, lavender, bay, roses, rue, sage, marjoram, and calamint were used to treat complaints of the head: comfrey was advised for lung complaints; the heart could be strengthened by borage, saffron, balm, basil, rosemary, and roses.

Herbs were also used extensively to sweeten the smell of homes, mixed with the rushes that covered the floors, sprinkled in cupboards, and heaped into bowls as pot-pourri. Perfumed waters were made from the many flowers which the Elizabethans loved. Life cannot always have been as sweet-smelling as they would have wished, and the scent of herbs and flowers helped to relieve the situation.

Nowhere was the use of herbs so important to a woman as in the treatment of female ailments and in the care of her children. Childbirth was an almost yearly occurrence for most women, but when life was so precarious very many children failed to survive early infancy, and producing a family was often difficult. To prevent miscarriage, rose petals were pounded until softened and then taken in honey along with rosemary and wild strawberries. A woman relieved her morning sickness with a drink made from tansy, also used in cases of threatened abortion. The pains of childbirth were thought to be alleviated by a brew of rue, with ground ivy and thyme useful for dealing with the afterbirth or inflammation of the uterus or breasts. Thyme could be used in a hot fomentation for abscesses and swellings. Wormwood was a useful herb for morning sickness, threatened miscarriage and the treatment of all fevers; puerperal fever was the great threat to the mother's health after childbirth. Newly born infants were baptized immediately in a cold christening chamber to ensure that they went straight to heaven if the birth had proved too much, and this practice often resulted in the mother swiftly following. Feverfew was a herb much used in childbirth, in the treatment of fevers, hysteria and difficult labours.

There was no generally recognized alternative to breast-feeding, although a primitive feeding bottle of cowhorn may

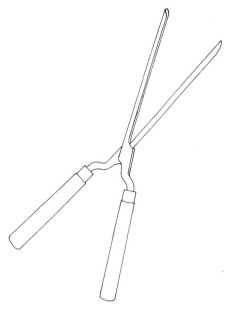

82 Goffering tongs
(*Tiverton Museum*)

draughts. The cradle had rockers under it for a mother to rock with her foot, no doubt while employing her hands in spinning or sewing. When old enough the child probably slept in a small trussing bed in its parents' room. Its childhood however was short, and it was trained at an early age to take its place in a busy home. Small stools and chairs for children, which probably came from wealthier homes, have been found. They are miniature versions of adult chairs, with nothing childish in their design, only in their size.

All toilet arrangements and washing facilities were of the most primitive sort, buckets and basins sufficing for every need. As carrying water from the nearest well must have been a full-time occupation for many people, it is not surprising that as little as possible was used for washing of any kind.

The flushed water-closet was in fact invented by Sir John Harington in 1596, but it seems that only the Queen thought it worth while to instal one. The idea did not become popular until the end of the 17th century, and then only to a limited extent. The Bayleaf farmhouse at Singleton in Sussex contains a small structure built on the side of the house at first-floor level which may have housed a garderobe or toilet, but it is not clear whether it emptied into an open cesspit, or down a drain into a river. The chamber vessel enclosed in a stool or box called a close-stool was found in some bedrooms.

have been used occasionally. Those who could afford it might employ a wet-nurse whose moral character was thought to be of more importance than the quality of her milk. It was thought that her vices could be passed on to the baby through her milk. Weaning took place as late as possible; Queen Elizabeth was not weaned until she was 13 months old. Infants were then fed on milk, whey and dairy produce.

On the whole Elizabethans treated children as small adults. When marriage took place at 15 and conditions of living were hard, growing up was a speedy process. Troublesome infants were soothed with dill water as they are today. Southernwood was a herb used for the treatment of the ailments of newborn infants and of their mothers. Until it could be let loose into the 16th century world of open fires, steaming cauldrons and roasting spits the child was placed in a baby-walker with wooden slatted sides that fitted under its arms, and kept it safe while its mother was at her work (79.3).

Rosemary was put under children's pillows to help them to sleep peacefully. The baby slept in a wooden or wicker cradle with a hood to protect it from

Laundering a ruff

For the most part laundry seems to have been done only once or twice a year. It was probably a sociable occasion when it did happen, much of it taking place out of doors on a fine day and in the river if there was one nearby (74). Neighbours would help each other with the heavier items, which would be washed by trampling them with the feet. They would be wrung by hand with the aid of a strong broom handle, which could be caught in one end of a blanket, the other end being fastened to the handle of a washtub. The articles would be smoothed with stones or a wooden bat. The lace and ruffs which were so popular, both for men and women, must have been laundered more frequently. These needed starching, a process which was introduced into England for this purpose about the middle of the 16th century, and also goffering tongs and irons.

Goffering tongs to make ruffs were like ordinary hair-curling tongs (82). Another early method of goffering was to lay the starched lace on a board carved into a large number of transverse ridges, each with a sharp edge. A roller with exactly matching ridges was passed over it, crimping the damp lace into shape. In the later goffering stack (83) the lace was threaded in and out of slots, held in place by a board clamped on the top, and placed in front of the fire to dry.

Later still the goffering machine (84.1) was used. Its fluted hollow rollers were heated by means of hot rods placed inside. A similar device, often wrongly described as a goffering iron (84.2), dealt with ribbons and edges still needing attention after using a flat iron; again it was heated by a hot rod or poker inside it. The

83 Goffering stack used to crimp lace etc; damp material wound round the loose wooden quills until dry (*Museum of English Rural Life*)

84.1 Goffering
machine,
19th century
(*Tiverton Museum*)

84.2 Iron for
smoothing ribbons
or lace, known as a
goffering iron
(*Welsh Folk Museum*)

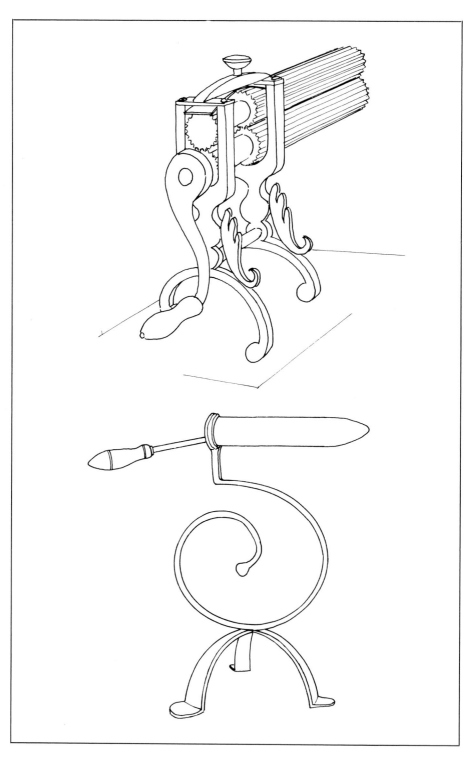

garment was then passed backwards and forwards over the smooth holder to smooth the edges that were still unpressed.

If the washing of clothes was not frequent, nor was the washing of bodies. Of course, the labour involved in making soap may have had something to do with this, to say nothing of the labour of fetching and carrying water from the well and heating it in a heavy cauldron.

London soap makers made three kinds of soap: speckled, which was the most expensive; white; and grey, which was the cheapest. There were many recipes for soap scented with herbs and flowers, and most soap was made at home. A lye was made from wood ash which had to be mixed with tallow (mutton fat) or some other similar grease to solidify it and help to make it scour. Nine kilogrammes (20 pounds) of lye was mixed with slightly less than a kilogramme (2 pounds) of fat, boiled for an hour and then strained and left to get cold, when it could be cut into cakes. This made a hard soap known as India, Venice, Marseilles, Castile and London soap.

In the farmhouse or cottage ordinary soap was made by mixing three parts of oak or beech ashes with one part of quicklime. Boiling water was added until the lye was strong enough to float an egg, and then the lye was drawn off. Three parts of lye to one of fat was boiled until it coagulated. Making a batch of soap must have been almost a day's work.

Before washing-soda came into use, lye was also used to soften the water for washing clothes. The lye dropper (86.1), was placed on top of a large tub, resting on a forked stick of hazel or maple. Twigs were arranged in the bottom of the dropper, a clean cloth was spread over them and white wood ash from the copper, brick oven or open fire was placed in it. Water was then poured on and allowed to drip through, washing out the alkaline salts as it did so. The lye so formed was strained through muslin to remove any ash. The lye dropper was also known as a leech or letch. The one illustrated is 50 centimetres square by 24 centimetres deep (19½ inches square by 9½ inches deep).

There is evidence at Pendean farmhouse, Sussex, dating from the end of the 16th century, that when the massive chimney was built in the centre of the house, providing fireplaces in three rooms, it also provided hot air to a cupboard of some sort at the side of the chimney, for airing or drying clothes. There was also a flue from this chimney providing a smoke chamber for curing bacon or other food for preserving for the winter. In another house of the period the builder went so far as to construct a hot-water system from a steam boiler in his kitchen. However, in true English fashion this was not to warm the house but to provide warmth for plants growing around it.

Of course, there were as usual those who could see little good in all these newfangled ideas. The Reverend William Harrison complained that the new houses being built (which incidentally have lasted for 400 years) were more like 'paper work, than substantial for continuance'. The absence of smoke from the fire in the middle of the room he regarded as a threat to health, and he complained that even in farmhouses straw pallets were being replaced by feather beds, and that no one now used a log of wood as a pillow. Pillows before this time were thought necessary only for women in childbirth. The Elizabethans were becoming soft.

Weaving her own sheets

The housewife had to sow flax and hemp in the spring and later prepare the fibre for making linen. If she could not make cloth from wool from her husband's sheep she had to use wool gathered from the hedgerow. From the humble cottage to the highest homes in the land women still spent all their spare time spinning, weaving and sewing. Most farmers' wives left behind a good supply of linen sheets, towels and napkins to be disposed of in their wills.

86.1 Lye dropper; lye was used to soften water and in making soap (*page 85*) (*Museum of English Rural Life*)

86.2 The bedroom of Kennixton farmhouse (*Welsh Folk Museum*)

Clothes, furnishings, wall hangings, and bed covers and curtains took priority, but more and more time was spent on embroidery in the 16th century. Everything that could be embroidered, was embroidered. Steel needles replaced drawn-wire ones about 1555 making the work easier and enabling finer work to be done. The lighter rooms in which to work must also have helped. When darkness came the light in the home was as it had always been: from candles for those who could afford them, and from rushlights for those who could not.

The evening meal was again most probably beer, bread and cheese served when work outside had finished. The beer was home-made, often flavoured with mace, nutmeg and sage. Both spices and extra materials for her sewing could only be obtained by the housewife at one of the seasonal fairs or from a passing pedlar.

Music was no doubt heard in the evenings in almost every home, for the Elizabethans were accomplished singers.

The bedroom of Kennixton Farmhouse at St Fagans is illustrated, with its four-poster bed and a raised child's bed (86.2). The intricately woven straw mats which form the underthatch of the roof are bound to the purlins with bramble strips, making a very pleasant ceiling in the bedroom.

One thing the farmer's wife could be assured of at the end of the day was a rest on down-filled pillows in the best feather bed her husband could afford. From inventories of the time it is clear that a four-poster bed was the most important item in the home and the most money was lavished on the bed itself and on its hangings. All this served to bring a little more warmth and comfort into the lives of its owners.

Working housewives: from a 16th-century playing card (*Mansell Collection*)

The Seventeenth-Century Home

As soon as labour began, all knots in the bedchamber were loosened ... the baby's first drink was a sip of water into which a red hot cinder had been dropped

The Saltonstall family: Des Granges
(*Tate Gallery*)

If a housewife had the luck to be provided with a new home near the end of the 17th century, it was likely to be closer to the compact and more easily run house of today than any we have considered so far.

New homes were of brick or stone, with small panelled rooms, and they were built for country squires, yeoman farmers, clergymen and merchants. The Stuart kings were not as generous in handing out rewards to their subjects as the Tudors had been, and the extensive building of large houses by the successful men of the previous century was halted to a great extent during the 17th century.

Homes were still being built in the older styles, such as Chastleton House in Oxfordshire, and in grander styles for the wealthy at Wilton and Hatfield, but the influences of Inigo Jones and Christopher Wren were eventually to be seen in the plain-fronted, symmetrically designed homes of which Mompesson House, Salisbury, Wiltshire is an early 18th century example.

The communal hall was shrinking fast to become a small entrance hall to the home, but then it was given a fine staircase leading to the upper storeys of the house. In the middle of the century some houses were for the first time built with the kitchen quarters partly underground, as at Coleshill in Berkshire. This was the beginning of the 'upstairs, downstairs' division that was to become usual in the following centuries.

The ornate and heavy furniture of the Elizabethans was changed for the simpler, lighter styles of the Jacobean period, more suited to the smaller rooms. This trend was furthered in the Cromwellian period, when carving and ornamentation were frowned upon by the Puritans as superfluous, and personal comfort such as the provision of cushions was looked upon as sinful. The joiner and turner came into their own and created the many pleasing furniture styles typical of the Jacobean period. Turning was approved of by the Puritans as being a form of decoration arising naturally from the skill of the craftsman.

Joined stools increasingly took the place of benches, and chairs became more common, especially the leather-covered, but unupholstered, chairs of the Commonwealth period. Their brass studs, being merely functional were an acceptable form of decoration. Stools however continued to be used for many years for sitting up to the table, a sturdy joined table which sometimes had a practical top that could be turned over, one side being polished, and the other a working surface. The folding gateleg table was also popular.

With the restoration of Charles II to the throne in 1660 luxury returned along with happier times and with any luck the housewife was allowed to have some stuffing in her leather chairs and cushions on her joined stools. She had more cupboards for storage and more things to put in them. A wardrobe was now what we know it to be, a cupboard for the storage of clothes.

90 The title page of Gervase Markham's *The English House-wife* (1683 edition) (*Museum of English Rural Life*)

THE
ENGLISH
Houſe-Wife,

CONTAINING

The inward and outward Vertues which ought to be in a Compleat Woman.

As her skill in *Phyſick*, *Chirurgery*, *Cookery*, *Extraction of Oyls*, *Banquuting ſtuff*, *Ordering of great Feaſts*, *Preſerving of all ſort of Wines*, *conceited Secrets*, *Diſtillations*, *Perfums*, *Ordering of Wool*, *Hemp*, *Flax* : Making *Cloath* and *Dying* ; The knowledge of *Dayries* : Office of *Malting* ; of *Oats*, their excellent uſes in Families : Of *Brewing*, *Baking*, and all other things belonging to an Houſhold.

A Work generally approved, and now the Ninth time much Augmented, Purged, and made moſt profitable and neceſſary for all men, and the general good of this NATION.

By G. Markham.

LONDON,
Printed for *Hannah Sambridge*, at the Sign of the *Bible* on *Ludgate-Hill*. 1683.

The chest of drawers changed from a chest with drawers at the bottom, to the kind we know today. In many cases the drawers were at first shyly hidden behind doors. The chair was probably the item of furniture that multiplied the fastest: easily moved styles, with light cane-filled backs, ladder backs and spindle backs.

Penalty for a nagging wife

The housewife was still being given endless advice by men, as to what were her duties and what should be her virtues. Gervase Markham, writing in 1615 (90), expressed the views of many: 'Your English housewife must be of chaste thought, stout courage, patient, untyred, watchful, diligent, witty and pleasant, constant in friendship, full of good neighbourhood, wise in discourse, but not frequent therein, sharp and quick of speech, but not bitter or talkative, secrete in her affairs, comfortable in her consailes, and skilful in all the working knowledges that belong to her vocation.'

If she was too frequent in her discourse, or too sharp and quick in her speech, she ran the danger of being ducked under water in a ducking stool or chair (91). Another punishment for 'scolds' was the brank or scold's bridle, an arrangement of iron hoops that passed over the head, with an iron piece that pressed into the mouth, holding down the tongue and forming a complete gag. The woman was paraded through the streets on a chain wearing this contraption.

The engraving from Markham's book (92) shows a kitchen of a farmhouse that had not been modernized, probably typical of many. Smoke is billowing into the room from the fire, the washing facilities look inadequate, and the hooks, which are everywhere, were the only means of storage for food and possessions. It has been suggested that those sitting round the fire kept on their hats to protect themselves from the danger of soot falling from the chimney.

The usual way for such a housewife to remove water from the clothes she was washing would have been to wring them by hand, or to wrap them round a wooden rolling pin and roll them with a mangle bat or board until the water was removed and the creases were gone. Considerable pressure was needed to do this. Oddly enough mangling boards were one of the many household objects carved by men as love tokens.

Apart from the early flat irons heated over the fire for ironing clothes (93.1), a box iron appeared in the 17th century, which was heated by a hot wrought-iron wedge placed inside (93.2). This was a type later made in brass.

Cooking was still done in a cauldron over the fire in many homes, and ladles (93.3) and flesh hooks for hooking out lumps of meat would hang alongside the fireplace as they had always done. As well as the salt box on the wall, there would be a knifebox (93.4), and in homes where candles were made or bought, there would hang a candle box. This was of wood,

91 Ducking chair
(*Ipswich Museum*)

92 Cottage interior from Markham's *The English House-wife* (*Museum of English Rural Life*)

sometimes carved; sometimes a rectangular box with a front that slid upwards, enabling the candles to be stored in an upright position, or else a metal cylindrical box with a curved lid of the type shown in the drawing (95.1). Both types were often painted. A kitchen such as the one shown was still likely to be lit by home-made rushlights. Salt was occasionally kept in the seat of a small fireside chair with a hinged lid.

The child in the engraving is held in a baby walker. Another type of baby minder consisted of an upright rod fitted into the floor at the base and into a beam overhead, the ring fitting round the child's body allowing it to move only within the radius of the baby minder or runner (95.3).

Of course the appearance of any farmhouse interior would depend to a large extent on how skilled the men were at working in wood during the long winter

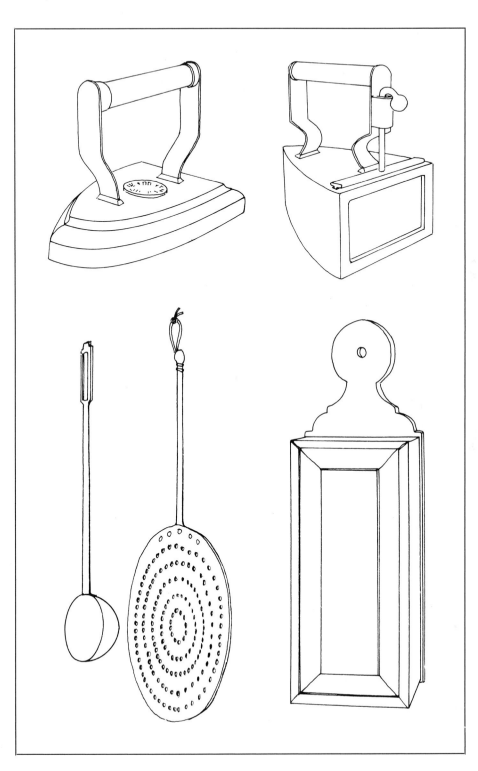

93.1 Flat iron
(*Tiverton Museum*)

93.2 Box iron
(*Tiverton Museum*)

93.3 Brass ladle and
skimmer to remove
cream

93.4 Knife box

evenings. The farmhouse of Townend at Troutbeck in Cumbria was completely rebuilt when George Browne, a yeoman farmer, married Susannah in 1623. The rebuilding was stipulated in the bride's marriage settlement. There the kitchen has been filled over the years with an assortment of fitted cupboards and drawers, incorporating even a long-case clock. Some of the cupboards in the house are built in as part of the walls. There are also chairs, children's chairs, a high chair and a cradle, all beautifully carved and home-made.

In many kitchens what had been the 'dresser', the table where the food was dressed, with shelves above, now became a compact unit of shelves with table and drawers in one piece of furniture: a dresser.

One of the objects carved in the 17th century with great attention to its appearance was a bible box to house the family bible. This box often had a sloping lid on which the bible could be rested for the daily reading. Many families started the day with prayers and bible readings at six in the morning. Few events can have made such a difference to the lives of the occupants of the home as the appearance in it of this book in the 17th century. It was an incentive for all to learn to read it for themselves, and once they had done this the influence on their lives was very great.

An independence of thought was spreading through the land, promoting discussion and dissension, and many different religious views developed that were frowned upon by the official Anglican Church. This in turn led to whole families, as well as individuals, seeking freedom to live, think and worship as they wished in the New World. They took their bibles with them, and in both countries the blank pages of the bible were used as a register of family marriages, births and deaths.

The wives of the men who emigrated were well fitted to cope with the pioneering life ahead. They were the end product of centuries of self-sufficiency in the home and as well as being proficient in the practical side of life, the religious and moral atmosphere of the home was dependent to a large extent on their strength of character. They had, at least, a strong background of daily prayer, religious reading and meditation to support them, whatever their religious views.

Many homes in the 17th century must have learned to cope with fear, trouble and hardship from time to time, for Anglicans, Puritans and Roman Catholics were all at loggerheads with one another. The Catholics suffered particular persecution.

At Harvington Hall, a moated manor house near Kidderminster, deep in the Worcestershire countryside, many alterations were made during the latter part of the 16th century and the beginning of the 17th by the Catholic family who lived there, which included the encasing of an older timber-framed structure in red brick to modernized its appearance. While this building was going on a unique series of secret hiding places was provided for persecuted priests. Ten such well-concealed hiding places have been discovered in the house so far: over bread ovens, under the floor of a garde-robe, hidden in staircases and behind wainscotting.

Smoking and tea drinking

Not only religious views were often under attack, but many of the habits that we take for granted today were looked upon with great disfavour when first introduced in the 17th century. James I called tobacco smoking 'A custom loathsome to the eye, hateful to the nose, harmful to the brain, dangerous to the lungs and in the black stinking fumes thereof nearest resembling the black stygian smoke of the pit that is bottomless.' In spite of this condemnation the popularity of smoking grew and to combat the stinking fumes many wives must have continually used a piperack (95.2) in which the long, clay churchwarden pipes were

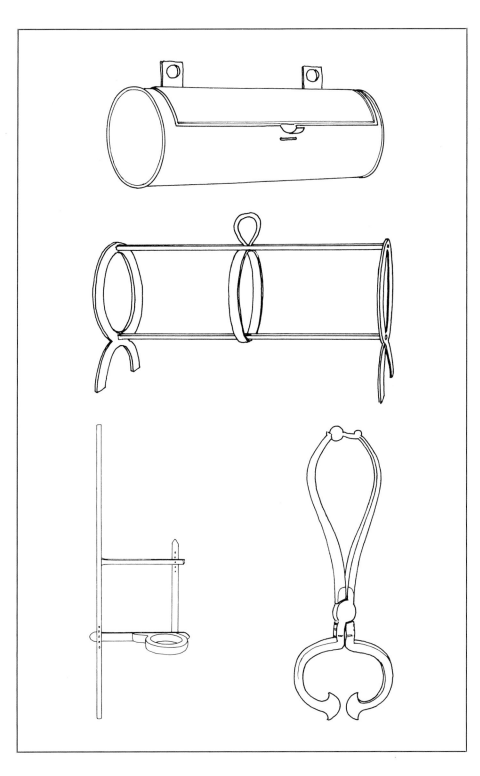

95.1 Metal candle box
(*page 92*)

95.2 Pipe rack

95.3 Baby minder or
runner (*page 92*)

95.4 Sugar cutters
(*page 96*)

placed and put in the fire, after which they came out comparatively clean.

Another condemned vice was tea drinking, but although tea was introduced, along with coffee and chocolate, about the middle of the century, it remained too expensive for popular consumption until the next century. Samuel Pepys notes in his diary that he tried a cup of China tea for the first time on September 25th, 1660. When it was drunk it was taken, as in China, from small handleless cups.

Towards the end of the century it was the fashion for the wealthy to take a drink of coffee or chocolate, with a little bread, at nine or ten in the morning: the beginning of 'elevenses'. Dinner was still at noon at the beginning of the century, but fashionable people dined later and later until in the 18th century dinner time was in the early afternoon.

A course at a formal dinner was composed of many dishes all put on the table at the same time. Forks were now used but were not overcommon. Samuel Pepys on April 4th, 1663 sat down to 'fricassee of rabbits, and chickens, a leg of mutton boiled, three carps in a dish, a great dish of a side of lamb, a dish of roasted pigeons, a dish of four lobsters, three tarts, a lamprey pie, a most rare pie, a dish of anchovies, good wine of several sorts, and all things mighty noble, and to my great content.' This was prepared by Mrs Pepys with the help of only one maid.

Much plainer meals with only one or two dishes were eaten on most days. Vegetables were still not very popular; pies made in what were called 'coffins' of pastry were much eaten, as well as many puddings. A Christmas pudding contained meat as well as eggs, peel, raisins, sugar and spices. Meat was also an ingredient of mince pies.

Many recipe books exist, often with religious maxims interspersed among the recipes. They were written with great care and amazing spelling by the housewives of the time, often containing recipes from friends, such as 'To make Sugar Crust –

Mrs Withers', 'To make Gooseberry Huff – Mrs D. Cruwys', 'To Butter Chicken – Mrs Cholwich'.

Mrs Cruwys' recipe for Gooseberry Huff is as follows:

Take a Quart of green Gooseberries boil them and pulp them thro' a Sieve, take the whites of 3 Eggs, beat them to a Froth, put it to the Gooseberries and beat it both together till it looks white, then take $\frac{1}{2}$ Pound of double refin'd Sugar, make it into a Syrrup with Spring Water, boyl it to a candy, let it be almost cold then put it to the Gooseberries and Eggs and beat all together till tis all froth, which put into Cup or Glasses – Codlings may be done the same way.

N.B. Eleven Ounces of Codlin pulp'd thro' a sieve is a proper quantity to the above Eggs and Sugar.

At the time there was no universally accepted standard of spelling, and everyone spelled as they wished and as the words sounded to them.

Whisking was done with birch twigs. Sugar was now imported from the West Indies in 10-lb sugar loaves which needed sugar cutters (95.4) to break them into pieces. A sweet eaten and much enjoyed since the Middle Ages was marchpane, a sort of marzipan that could be coloured and made into many shapes.

Ale for breakfast

Large quantities of home-brewed ale was the most popular general drink, consumed in tankards (97) from breakfast time onwards. Often the ale was spiced and heated in a copper boot-shaped container, the toe of which could be pushed into the embers of the fire. Quantities of cider were made, especially in the west country. The wealthy imported wine from abroad and the not-so-wealthy made quantities of home-made wine from the herbs and flowers of the countryside.

The housewife must have spent many hours preparing wines, lotions and herbal cures in her still-room, and collecting flowers and herbs must have been time-consuming in itself. They had to be collected at the correct hour of the day and at the right stage of growth for maximum effect. She had to be careful with her curative skills, especially if she was an old woman living alone, otherwise she might be thought to be a witch and it would be back to the ducking stool, or worse. Witches were imagined everywhere in the 17th century and their persecution reached a peak in the middle of the century when 200 witches were executed in the eastern counties of England alone.

A Dorset recipe, for insomnia, runs as follows:

To caus sleep. Take a nuttmegg and a little large mace pound this small and mix them wth a little treakle put them in a linnin bagg warm it and lay it to the temples.

Remedies to assist in childbirth were many:

A receit for a woman tht cannot be delivered. Goody Wilsheirs. Tak a yolk of a new led egge and put 2 pennyworth of saffaron finly beaten into it and a little sugar and so give in her mouth and after let her drink mace ale or burnt claret.

If a woman hath hard travel. Give her hisop water to drink sweettened with sugar. If she be very ill boyle hisop in water and sweeten it with sugar, it will bring on pain and caus her to be delivered.

As can be imagined there were many customs connected with childbirth. As soon as labour began all knots in the bedchamber were loosened. The midwife always wrapped the baby in an old piece of cloth as its first garment and was careful to see that its first journey was up and not down even if she had to stand on a chair with the baby in her arms. The baby's first drink was a sip of water into which a red-hot cinder had been dropped.

Cooking was still done over an open

97 Pewter tankard

fire (98). Only at the end of the century in larger homes was an early form of range introduced, with a confined fire and adjacent ovens.

The spit could now be turned by a mechanical jack instead of by hand, either by using a system of weights and gears or by a smoke-jack which was worked by the rising heat and smoke of the fire. The jack was attached by long chains or cords to work a wheel at one end of the spit (99.1).

The kitchen fire was not allowed to go out, because lighting it in the early morning was so difficult. It was covered at night, as it had been in the Middle Ages for safety during the 'couvre-feu' or curfew laws, then revived in the morning with bellows, a household necessity for centuries. Lighting a fire before the invention of matches was a tedious business, involving a tinder box sometimes with a candle-socket on the lid, with a steel and flint which were struck together until a spark appeared which fell onto the piece of tinder or charred linen (99.2). This precious spark had to be very gently blown upon until it glowed and a thin piece of wood could be lit from it, which in turn could light a candle or rushlight. It is not

surprising that a beaker of ale and a piece of bread was the usual breakfast.

When she was not occupied in the still-room or kitchen a great deal of a house-wife's time was spent in the dairy, a room situated on the coolest side of the house, with small windows, thick walls and a stone or slate flagged floor. Here the milk was set in wide wooden or earthenware pans and the cream that was skimmed off was churned into butter in a plunger-type wooden churn. This was a laborious process, taking at least half an hour before the butter would 'come'. During this time charms were muttered and witches kept at bay to prevent mishaps. Later in the 17th century the butter was made in a barrel-churn revolved by a turned handle.

The butter next had to be washed (99.3), salted and stored for later use or made into small shapes, after being weighed on wooden scales. Butter 'hands' were used to shape the butter, which was then stamped with a wooden butter mould. These moulds were among many beautifully carved wooden utensils in the home, a housewife often having her own particular stamp by which her butter could be identified in a market (100). Cheesemaking was a further task in the dairy (101) and the cheese press (102) required considerable physical strength, something a farmer had to take into account when choosing a wife.

A spinning wheel was now found in almost every home. Often there was one wheel for wool and another for flax, the latter used to make thread for the many homespun sheets, tablecloths, napkins and towels which appear in the inventories of the time. A great amount of time must have been spent in this occupation. A yeoman's household could boast as many as 20 pairs of sheets.

The weaving was usually done by a visiting weaver or by someone in the village who had their own loom. The flax was locally grown or home grown and its preparation, by the women, was a long and

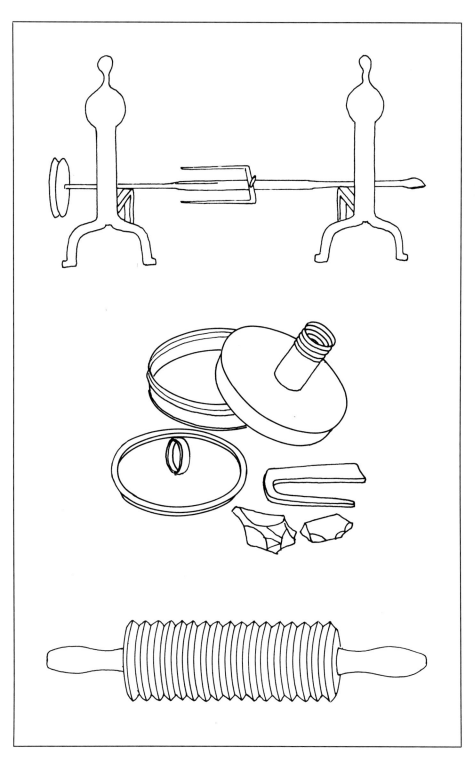

99.1 Pronged roasting spit with wheel at one end to which a chain or cord was attached (*page 97*)

99.2 Tinder box with flint, steel and disc to quench the tinder 10 cm (4 in) across (*page 97*)

99.3 Butter worker, for rolling the butter to remove water 30 cm (12 in) long

100 Carved butter
moulds (*Page 98*)
(*Welsh Folk Museum*)

smelly business. The seed was sown in
April and the plants had to be well weeded
by hand. They were harvested in August
and then had to be soaked so that the fibres
decomposed. This was known as 'retting'.
Flax retting pools were found near cottages, but the smell and contamination of
the water often caused complaints. The
fibres were then dried and went through
the scutching process whereby they were
beaten to separate the woody and fibrous
parts. Later scutching took place in mills.

A material often mentioned in inventories is linsey-woolsey, which was a
mixture of wool and linen. The coarser
fibres from nearer the rind were spun into
'towen' sheets, sometimes called canvas.
Poorer people used hemp.

As the century progressed it was increasingly possible to buy ready-made
material in towns, and the tailor and
shoemaker appeared in the village in
addition to the miller and baker of the
previous century. All these village wor-

kers were farmers as well. The increasing
use of ready-made materials was, not
surprisingly, just another step in the
emancipation of women frowned upon by
the clergymen of the day.

Children dressed as adults

As well as spinning, women were busy
at their embroidery. Little girls made their
first samplers to practise a variety of
stitches by the time they were seven or
eight. Women wore elaborately embroidered petticoats and skirts were
looped up or open at the front to show
them. The padded roll worn round the
hips under the dress, known as a farthin-
gale, which had been such an exaggerated
and popular style at the end of the
Elizabethan period, lasted until about
1620, and was superseded by skirts which
hung gracefully from a new high waistline.
At the same time the large starched ruffs
were replaced by large lace-trimmed collars which fell over the shoulders. Children

101 The dairy at Mary Arden's farmhouse at Wilmcote, Stratford-on-Avon (*page 98*) (*The Shakespeare Birthplace Trust: Jarrolds of Norwich*)

were dressed in miniature versions of their parents' clothes (103).

Hair styles became very elaborate with ringlets and curls, and after the Restoration many women adopted wigs, already fashionable for men. Many people were put off wearing wigs by the fear of infected hair during times of plague.

The apron of the Elizabethan housewife became part of a fashionable lady's attire in the middle of the century. The apron started as a plain lawn one with perhaps a lace edge, but ended up by the end of the century as an elaborate piece of silk or taffeta, heavily ornamented with ribbons and embroidery, with gold or silver lace edges.

Under their petticoats women tied pockets on tapes round their waists, in which they hid their money for security. Their less important possessions they carried in ornamental bags, sometimes tying these on a ribbon round their waists as well.

102 Cheese press
(page 98)
(Welsh Folk Museum)

Frequent funerals

Beautiful gloves were worn by both men and women, and were often given as presents, as gifts to everyone at weddings and to mourners at funerals. The latter occasions were frequent, but attendance at them was a necessary duty, taken very seriously. With plague, persecution, smallpox and civil war occupying so much of the century, one never knew when one's own funeral might not be the next. The whole home was draped in black after a death, and mourning clothes were worn for several years, often including black night clothes.

Apart from these sad occasions the Stuart home must have been pleasant to view. The panelling and oak furniture would not have had the somewhat dark and dreary appearance it does today. When new the oak was a golden colour and only darkened with use and age. Floors were now boarded and the rushes had become rush matting. Travelling painter–stainers occasionally stopped at the home and painted whole rooms or small pictures on the wall panels.

The parlour was often still the sleeping quarters for the parents of the family and contained a four-poster bed (103), with slender posts instead of the heavily carved ones of the previous century. Entertaining was done in the parlour, in spite of the presence of the bed which was in fact probably one of the few comfortable places to sit. It had a rush mattress resting on cords stretched across the bed frame, with a feather mattress on top.

Toilet arrangements were still confined to chamber pots and close-stools, though the rich might have a privy in some secluded corner of the house. In this respect the new homes were not so advanced as those of the Middle Ages.

During the 17th century there was a gradual immigration of Dutch and French craftsmen who were experts in cotton printing, a process well established on the Continent but not in England. They printed the first chintzes which were used

103 Women embroidering in a parlour; there is a bed in the room. Les Femmes à table en l'absence de leurs maris: Abraham Bosse (*Victoria and Albert Museum*)

for furnishings, by applying designs with a wooden block on to rough hand-woven canvas. The printing of these chintzes at Richmond, Bow and Old Ford brought great prosperity to the country. But for the most part bed hangings and other furnishings were still embroidered.

The homes of many yeoman farmers increased in prosperity after the Civil War. Such items as rugs, desks, mirrors, silver and chairs found their way from ruined Royalist homes into the houses of the farmers, who had kept out of the conflict. These men were surprisingly well read, with a small library of books, and were quite capable of making up their minds over questions of religion and politics. There is no reason to believe that their wives did not keep up with them in this respect. The Quaker ladies in particular were women of strong, independent minds, helped as they were by the Quaker doctrine of the equality of men and women and freedom of thought.

The first books on household matters written by women for women appeared in the 17th century. They were produced for the many wives who wished to improve their capabilities and move up in the world. Many daughters of wealthy yeoman farmers married the sons of local squires and needed to know how to manage their servants, and an increasing number of women wished to become housekeepers for other women. By the end of the century the women in country districts were increasingly drawn to life outside their homes both in London and the bigger towns.

Many women had had to defend their homes without their husbands' help during the Civil War. Many had been under siege for long periods. It is not surprising that their husbands complained that things were not quite the same in the home on their return from the war.

The Eighteenth-Century Home

. . . their hair had often been dressed in an elaborate style many weeks before and not touched since, but they did have bejewelled gold rods to scratch their heads . . . one aristocratic lady had a miscarriage on discovering mice in her hair

The poor parson's wife had worse things to worry about than preserving her hair style; she might well have to feed her family on an income of as little as £20 a year: JOURNEYMAN PARSON WITH A BARE EXISTENCE: Robert Dighton, *The Fotomas Index*

Saltram House near Plympton in Devon is a typical 18th-century stately home, but its mistress was not the wealthy, fashionable lady portrayed by the literature, plays and paintings of the time. Theresa Parker did not paint her face excessively, nor powder her hair and dress it several feet high. She did not occupy her days with gossip, nor was she unfaithful to her husband or involved in domestic scandals. The truth is that such people were a comparatively small minority and not typical of many country women who, whatever their position, viewed the activities of people of fashion with amusement and even contempt.

Theresa was 25 when she married John Parker, MP for Devon, in 1769, and came to live at Saltram. By the time she died in 1775 she had left a marked impression on the house and on all with whom she had associated. From the many letters written by, and to all members of her family, it seems that the entertaining expected of the owners of such houses as Saltram did not give her any great pleasure, although she did her share, but she is probably more typical of many women of the time than one might suppose.

She appears to have been an intelligent, sensitive and artistic woman who was principally concerned with the welfare of her family; well read and used to corresponding and discoursing with the many people of influence and talent with whom she came into contact, all of whom formed a high opinion of her. She loved Saltram dearly and played a large part in choosing designs for the alterations and furnishings made in her time. She looked after the affairs of the estate while her husband was away from home, and took an active interest in his plans for agricultural improvements. She probably had more to do with choosing the many paintings for the house than did her husband and she was a collector of the porcelain and Wedgwood and the delicate china figures produced at this peak period of 18th-century craftsmanship.

She was obviously one of those women, growing in numbers by the end of the century, who were increasingly tired of being considered merely as objects of fashion with no minds of their own. They thought women should be as well educated as men and worked hard to bring this about. A group of the more articulate of them held parties in London where the guests were expected to engage in conversation and discussion, rather than gossip and cards, and were not expected to dress in high fashion. It was said that it was not even necessary for a man to wear black silk stockings to attend; blue worsted stockings would suffice. These intellectual women of the 18th century, led by Mrs Elizabeth Montagu, became known as the 'blue stockings'.

At this time many women from country homes were increasingly drawn towards the life of leisure offered by London and the other large towns which were growing so fast. Theatres, shops, balls, assemblies and pleasure gardens provided pastimes that for the first time made country life seem dull in comparison.

The age of the country house
The Parkers rented a house in London for the season and while John Parker had to attend Parliament, but both of them preferred country life, as did the majority of those who built the many country homes of the time. This was the most glorious period for the building of our country houses in England, and those who did not build anew enclosed their older Tudor buildings with completely new facades of classical design. Grand pillared porches became essential for the front of the house, with east and west wings added wherever possible.

Every country house of any importance had to have its orangery, summerhouse, stables, hot-houses and greenhouses, and the grounds themselves were completely transformed. Gone were the formal beds and paths of the two previous centuries. The land around the house was land-

scaped, with sweeps of open country and strategically placed trees, lakes and small buildings to attract the eye in a manner that came to be associated with the name of Capability Brown, who replanned so many famous gardens at this time.

The small buildings were specially built cottages, temples, small castles and follies of all kinds. Probably the gardens at Stourhead in Wiltshire are the best example of this style, except that the rhododendrons planted there at a later date would not have fitted into the 18th century plan. The colours were meant to give the subdued effect of the romantic landscape paintings so admired at the time.

Inside the houses rooms were transformed. Anything further from the heavy, wood-laden rooms of the 16th and 17th centuries is difficult to imagine. The furniture was now of mahogany or walnut, not oak, and made by a cabinet-maker from books of design bearing such famous names as Chippendale, Hepplewhite and Sheraton.

John Parker was fortunate enough to employ the services of the Scottish designer Robert Adam, the greatest exponent of the neo-classical style of the 18th century. One of the most beautiful rooms designed by Adam at Saltram is the dining room. In pale green and white, all is grace and lightness in this room. Adam designed everything in it, as he liked to do: walls, ceilings, furnishings, carpet and ornaments right down to the door handles. He employed well-known painters to paint oil paintings that fitted perfectly into his design for walls and ceiling, even including miniature paintings on the edges of the side tables. The carpet reflects the ceiling in design and was specially woven at Axminster.

The dining room of the 18th century did not have a large table in the centre, but a series of small tables that stood either outside the room or round the walls, only being moved into the centre of the room when needed. The appearance of the room was important, not the purpose for which it was used.

Before entering the dining room, visitors would have come through the entrance hall and then through a small morning room and the velvet drawing room (two rooms used for the daily life of the family when no visitors were present), then into the spacious saloon also designed by Robert Adam.

This great drawing room is entered through double doors and after the smaller rooms must have impressed the visitors quite as much as it was meant to. The spaciousness, the light, the great wall mirrors, the paintings by Sir Joshua Reynolds, the Adam-designed settees and chairs arranged round the walls, are typical of the neo-classical age. The room was lit by candles in tortoise-shell and ormolu candelabra, which stand on carved gilt-wood stands again designed by Adam. Silver candle snuffers on small silver trays would have been nearby to keep the wicks perpetually trimmed.

Just as the Elizabethans of wealth and position had to have their long galleries, so the owners of large country houses in the 18th century had to have their saloons in which they could entertain the high society of the age.

Diners at Saltram were lucky because the kitchen quarters were close enough to the dining room for there to be some hope of the food being reasonably hot when it reached the table. Usually in such a house they were as far away from the elegant living rooms as possible. Lukewarm food must have been the order of the day, although closed trolleys were in use to wheel the food to the dining room. In the next century these were sometimes heated by gas.

Cleaning the saucepans
The food was prepared in a glowing 'batterie de cuisine' found on the shelves around all the large kitchens of the time. The kitchen at Saltram (109) contains some 600 pieces of copper, tinned internally. All of them had to be cleaned with

sand, which was the only scouring powder. Verdigris in the copper pans was a great danger, and Mrs Hannah Glasse, a prolific writer of cookery and household management books of the 18th century, reported that a whole family had died from this cause. Household books increased in number through the century and slowly standards of household hygiene improved. All shapes and sizes of copper saucepans were used for preparing the large number of dishes served. Particularly noticeable are the copper moulds for desserts and sweets, from very large to minute.

A great deal of whisking and pounding still went on in the kitchen, but the accent was on the elegance of the finished product and the dishes from which it was served

and eaten. These dishes, the silverware on the table, including the cutlery (forks were now in daily use), and the glasses from which the wine was drunk are some of the most beautiful ever designed and, along with the setting in which the meal was eaten, have contributed to the 18th century being well named 'The Age of Elegance'.

When all this has been said one must add that the Chippendale sideboard also housed chamber-pots (beautifully designed of course) for the use of the diners during the hours of eating and drinking, the drinking being on a prodigious scale. Elegant perfume burners stood in the corners to mask the fact that a bath before dinner for the sumptuously dressed diners, or even a wash, was unlikely. The ladies'

109 The 18th century kitchen at Saltram House, Devon, with sugar loaves on the table and glass fly catchers on the right hand cupboard (*National Trust*)

fans were used to hide their mouths and dissipate bad breath, and their hair had often been dressed in an elaborate and powdered style many weeks before and not touched since, except for the application of more powder (powder rooms for this purpose were well named), but they did have bejewelled gold rods to scratch their heads.

The meat and poultry were probably tough, having walked every mile of the long way to market, and frequently bad as well because of poor storage facilities.

Often the chimney smoked because it was designed to enhance the outside appearance of the house and not primarily as an efficient means of removing smoke from the fire. A typical comment on the times was 'At court last night, there was dice, dancing, crowding, sweating and stinking in abundance as usual.'

Efforts were made to overcome many of these disadvantages as the century progressed. Hotplates of cast iron with their own independent fires were installed to keep food and plates warm until they were served. A screen with shelves could be pulled in front of the fire for the same purpose.

Food was probably freshest in country homes where it came from the garden or the estate. In the towns it cannot always have been too fresh, especially the milk, which was brought round by milkmaids with a yoke over their necks. A heavy bucket of milk hung from each side of the yoke and these buckets were often uncovered. Cans of various sizes hung round the buckets to dispense the milk.

More vegetables were eaten than in the past, including root vegetables, greens and potatoes. Lord Townshend, known as 'Turnip Townshend' was one of the country landowners who devoted himself to the development of new and improved crops. He demonstrated how large amounts of turnips could be grown, both as a food for people and as a winter feed for cattle, enabling them to be kept through the winter to provide fresh meat, rather

110.1 Copper warming pan

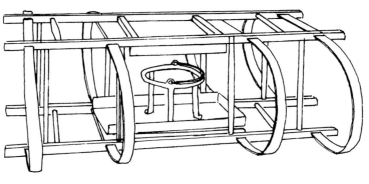

110.2 Bed-waggon, a heated contraption for warming the bed on cold nights, 1.2 m (4 ft) wide

than all meat for winter use having to be salted down. Meat was still served highly spiced to disguise its poor quality, and the spices were still expensive and kept under lock and key in spice boxes or cupboards.

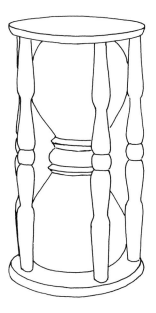

111 Hour glass

Water cans and chamber pots

Baths were no doubt taken in their rooms by some ladies, but the bath water and all washing water had to be heated in the kitchen over the fire and carried a long way to the bedrooms in a multitude of copper cans, the dirty water eventually having to be carried down again. Piped water to town houses was sometimes installed in the second half of the century, but it was only available for short periods during the day and perhaps only several times a week, and it was advisable to let it stand for the sediment to settle. Close-stools and chamber pots were still the only toilet facilities.

The dressing room at Saltram has Chinese wallpaper, still on the walls today and probably one of the earliest papers from the Far East in existence in England. Wallpapers in bedrooms had been known since the end of the 17th century. In the adjoining bedroom, hung with Chinese paintings on silk or cotton and furnished with a Chippendale bed and furniture in the Chinese fashion so popular in the late 18th century, Theresa read her books, practised her drawing and arranged her china collection.

The bed would have been heated by a copper warming pan(110.1).The hinged lid opened and there was an iron liner inside which was filled with hot embers of wood or charcoal. Later warming pans were made to be filled with hot water. To warm and air a large bed a bed-waggon was used (110.2). It was a large contraption which held a pan of hot embers, the bedclothes being protected by the wooden frame with a sheet of iron above and below the embers.

Airing rooms and beds was a constant worry, colds and fevers so often proving fatal. Theresa Parker's short stay at Salt-ram ended with her death after the birth of her second child. She had taken great care of herself, both before and after the birth, doing all the things customary at the time, such as not using her eyes for a month after the birth for reading, writing or sewing. In spite of all possible care and attention she died after having the fever that so often accompanied childbirth, followed by a cold.

The photograph (112) of the bedroom at 7, Charlotte Square in Edinburgh shows the four-poster bed, with its hangings embroidered by Lady Mary Hog. It has a little pocket above each pillow to hold a watch. Watches, barometers and clocks, particularly long-case clocks, appeared with increasing frequency as essential items in wealthier homes. Those who could not afford them still had to time their activities and their cooking with the aid of an hour-glass (111). These were also used by preachers to time their sermons, which had been very long since the 17th century.

Two innovations in the home life of wealthier 18th-century women have re-mained with us ever since: the coffee break in the morning and a light lunch eaten at midday to stave off hunger pangs. Dinner

112 18th-century bed at 7, Charlotte Square, Edinburgh (*page 111*) (*The National Trust for Scotland*)

was moving to a later and later hour, from 3 o'clock at the beginning of the century to 5 p.m. or later by the beginning of the 19th century.

The popularity of coffee drinking grew apace with the opening of increasing numbers of coffee shops in London and the larger cities. These were male preserves, and were great meeting places for gossip and discussion. They served tea and chocolate as well as coffee. By the middle of the century tea, bread and cheese had become the staple diet of the poor. This at least was better than the large quantities of cheap, poor-quality gin that the poor had consumed up till then. Kitchens in large establishments had tea in large canisters clearly labelled 'Kitchen Tea' and 'Best Tea', although the tea-making ceremony was more often than not carried out in the sitting room, made by the lady of the house herself from tea kept in her own locked tea caddy. The family tealeaves were often used again by the servants, and then sold to the poor at the back door.

This tea-drinking habit resulted in many more acquisitions for the home. There had to be small tables, teapots, teacups, saucers, plates and spoons for this new pastime, and in the 18th century these were all beautifully designed by master craftsmen. All this equipment evolved during the century. At first silver teapots were used but the tea was drunk from Chinese tea bowls (without handles) imported from China. By about 1750 globular porcelain teapots replaced the silver ones. Porcelain teacups, as we know them, began to be manufactured in England and were used alongside the tea bowls until about 1815, when the practice of using the bowls in the Chinese manner was finally abandoned.

Mashing the tea

By the end of the century Josiah Wedgwood was producing pottery in such quantities that it was brought within the reach of many homes. The pewterware in constant use in the previous centuries was now relegated to the kitchen for the use of the servants.

The terms formerly used for brewing beer attached themselves to the ritual of tea making, and the tea was said to be 'brewed' or 'mashed', the latter term being originally used for pouring boiling water onto the malt in brewing ale.

Coffee-mills (113.1) were now needed in the kitchen. It seems that every increase in the standard of living was accompanied by an increase in the number of articles needed to do the work there, and all of them needed cleaning.

Some jobs in the kitchen became easier. Spits could now be worked by a clockwork spit jack wound up by a key (113.2). Here the joint was suspended underneath and revolved vertically, instead of horizontally. Vertical cooking became necessary when the fire was confined in a narrower space behind bars, this in turn being the result of the use of coal.

A Dutch oven (114.1) became popular for this type of vertical cooking. It was a

113.1 Coffee mill

polished metal screen put in front of the fire to radiate heat. It had a polished brass 'bottle jack' above, also wound up with a key. The meat was turned four times to the left and then slowly back to the right. The dripping ran into the well in the floor, out through little holes in the top of the well and into a dripping tin below. It was thus strained ready for use. The oven had a door at the back so that the meat could be inspected and basted. Meat cooked very well by this method.

Toast could be made on an iron toaster, adjustable to the height of the fire (114.2). Those who still cooked on an open fire, known as the 'down hearth', could make

113.2 Clockwork spit jack
(*Welsh Folk Museum*)

114.1 Dutch oven with clockwork jack (*page 113*) (*Welsh Folk Museum*)

114.2 Adjustable iron toaster (*page 113*) (*Museum of English Rural Life*)

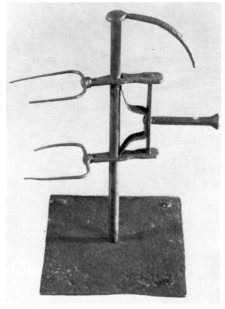

toast or roast a small piece of meat on a 'down hearth toaster' (115.1), with attached dripping pan. Salted and smoked meat still hung from overhead racks in the kitchen, but the cook could be sure of having a fresh fowl ready for use by keeping it in an iron cage in the kitchen until she was ready to deal with it (115.2).

Keeping food fresh and free from the attentions of vermin had been a problem for centuries. Kitchens were usually painted blue, a colour which traditionally kept away flies. In the 18th century glass flycatchers were used, narrow-necked and decanter-shaped, standing on tiny glass knobs to keep them half an inch from the surface on which they were placed. They closed at the top with a stopper, and the open base had the glass turned inwards, so that the flies could enter from the bottom, lured by beer, jam or sweetened water, but could not escape. Parson Woodforde in his 19th-century diary records that he served his guests a ham, the major part of which had been entirely eaten by flies.

Rats and mice were a constant problem dealt with first by cats and then by a variety of ingenious home-made mousetraps devised over the centuries, including a 'deadfall' type of trap, which killed immediately by the falling of a heavy wooden block. Others had wires to strangle mice or rats, or used walking-the-plank methods for drowning them (117.1–3). Bread was stored in crates and nets hanging from the ceiling as a 'prevention is better than cure' method.

Hygiene in the kitchen was not easy to achieve, and not until the end of the century was it thought particularly necessary. A kitchen in the late 17th or early 18th century might have had a stone sink with metal taps for water which had to be pumped from outside, but the flow could not be regulated. Only occasionally was a housewife lucky enough to have a pump in her kitchen. Some large country homes had ice-houses in the grounds for the storage of food. These were underground vaults kept cool by ice collected from

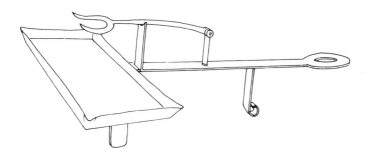

115.1 Down-hearth
toaster
(*Tiverton Museum*)

frozen lakes and ponds.

Most people still used wood for their fires, particularly for cooking. The use of sea coal (so called because it was largely transported by sea), increased all the time, especially in towns and large houses, but where it was still obtainable, wood was preferred. For one thing it was easier to light. Small hand-picked coal was always used for a good roasting fire and was kept in straw baskets, to make carrying as easy as possible.

Charcoal was used for some cooking, as it had been since Roman times, but it was not considered healthy. Parson Wood-forde made a special mention of the fact in his diary that his niece Nancy was over-come by giddiness while making jam on a charcoal stove although she had kept the door open all the time.

A new type of iron for ironing clothes also used charcoal (118.1). This needed considerable care in its handling. The charcoal was placed inside and a hole in the back acted as a ventilator, and also as a place to insert the nozzle of a bellows. The pumping of the bellows made the charcoal burn more vigorously, although if the laundress had the strength she could increase the heat of the iron by swinging it to and fro in her hand. The iron had a heat shield to protect the hand and a funnel to carry away the heat.

Ironing, a hot and tiring occupation, was now becoming more necessary. The introduction of new and lighter materials

115.2 Iron cage
for fowl
(*Ipswich Museum*)

for clothing made laundry work more frequent. No doubt the sewing of iron holders to protect the hands from hot irons was an increasingly necessary evening occupation. Ordinary flat irons now came in a variety of sizes, including very small ones only 5 to 8 centimetres (2 or 3 inches) long for ironing small pleats and tucks (118.2). The traditional method of testing the temperature of an iron was to spit on it and observe the time it took for the spittle to evaporate.

In large households the dirty linen was saved for a month, or perhaps three for a large wash, but in smaller families with less linen it was of necessity more frequent and extra help was employed to cope with it.

Cotton fabrics and muslins were imported into the country and women increasingly bought material for their clothes instead of making their own cloth. Even country housewives could buy ready-made material from travelling salesmen and at the local fairs, though spinning wheels were still hard at work in many homes.

The London fashions

In 1801 *The Lady's Magazine* reported on Queen Charlotte's birthday, noting that the use of powder had completely gone out among the ladies and that their hair was chiefly dressed naturally in braids or curls with bandeaux of gold or embroidery running across in front with diamond ornaments. Feathers were universal including white ostrich, bird of paradise, pheasant and macaw plumes.

Readers of the magazine learned that London fashions included walking dresses in lilac muslin with full sleeves in white muslin and lace, the dress cut low round the bosom and worn with a handkerchief, accompanied by a white-and-lilac bonnet to match, ornamented with a large round feather fixed in front to hang over the left side. The favourite colours for the end of the century were lilac, buff, yellow and pink, with feathers and flowers of all kinds worn as ornaments. Straw hats with

flowers, feathers and ribbons were worn with these pretty dresses.

For the first time voices were raised in protest at the amount of time and effort spent by women on embroidery. It was said that the hours spent by children and young ladies bending over needlework were detrimental to their health. *The Female Spectator*, a woman's magazine of the 1740s, said that it was not now necessary for wealthy young ladies to occupy themselves producing large quantities of unwanted linen. It was more important for them to learn to be good conversationalists and women of fine taste. The preparation of too many preserves was also thought to be unnecessary.

Young ladies were now sent away to schools where they were taught accomplishments like French, dancing and music, including the pianoforte by the end of the century. When they returned to their country homes this education only served to make them more discontented than ever with the boredom of their lives, now that they were not fully occupied with domestic duties.

Many women continued to make their own clothes and most of them, who had not the money or desire to buy the many doubtful patent medicines on the market, still produced their own home remedies.

But families in remote country districts, however great, were helpless when faced with serious illness. In 1772 at Walhampton, near Lymington in Hampshire, Sir Harry Burrard intended to celebrate the debut of his only daughter Laura at the age of 18 by holding a ball in her honour. The night before the ball the house guests were practising some country dances, when it was discovered that Laura was missing. She was found upstairs in her own room lying in a pool of blood, dying from a broken blood vessel. An old servant of the family rode non-stop through the night to London over the appalling roads of the time, completing the 168 miles in record time, to fetch some remedy that had been suggested, but he was too late to save her.

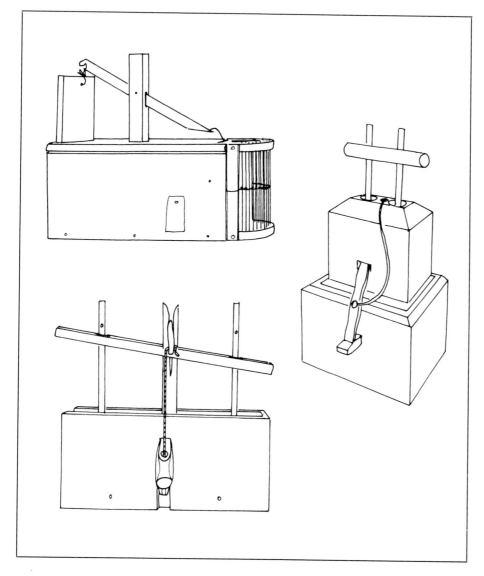

117.1–3 Three types
of mousetrap
(*page 114*)

The guests for the ball found themselves taking part in a funeral procession instead. It was held at night, a usual time for fashionable funerals. The mourners, carrying torches, walked from Walhampton up the hill to Lymington Church. The attendance at funerals at this time was usually predominantly male, but when a young girl died unmarried she was followed to her grave by women and young people dressed in white. This was known as a maiden funeral. The coffin was covered with a white pall and white flowers.

Although Walhampton was a house visited by George III and his family, only one coach was kept there, and there were only two in the whole district. When a ball was given these coaches were sent round to collect any ladies who were unable to ride their horses or forest ponies, the usual mode of transport.

Lady Burrard, Laura's mother, like

118.1 Charcoal iron
(page 115)
(Tiverton Museum)

118.2 Tiny iron, only
5–8 cm (2–3 in), for
tucks and pleats
(page 116)
(Tiverton Museum)

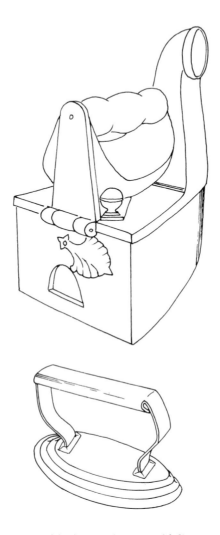

most wealthy housewives, would dispense herbal remedies and medicines to the poor of the district, as there was no local doctor for them, but in the case of very serious accident or illness she was powerless and death was inevitable.

Although medical and scientific knowledge made much progress during the 18th century, the medical practitioners left much to be desired. Quacks and many doubtful patent remedies were everywhere. One of the most fashionable doctors who attended George III had no medical qualifications at all. Bleeding the patient was still the most usual treatment, and remedies using worms and snails were not unusual.

The plague had almost died out in England since the last severe outbreak in 1665 and the disease most feared, particularly by women as it might well leave them hideously disfigured for life, was smallpox. Lady Mary Wortley Montagu, when in Turkey as the wife of the ambassador, found that the Turks had a method of inoculation against smallpox and had her own son inoculated while in Turkey and her daughter on her return to England. She suffered a torrent of abuse from the press and the Church and from doctors, but managed to get royal support, and the two daughters of the Princess of Wales were inoculated.

Eventually Dr Edward Jenner performed the first successful vaccination using cow-pox, and vaccination centres were set up all over England at the beginning of the 19th century. Vaccination was made compulsory in 1853. Theresa Parker was one of the courageous women who had their children inoculated when the process was still the subject of much controversy.

Deadly cosmetics

Even if they did not catch smallpox, many fashionable ladies managed to kill themselves off at an early age by the cosmetics they used. A white skin was considered essential. Masks were worn to avoid freckles and pole screens kept the heat of the fires from delicate complexions. They applied deadly preparations containing mercury and white lead to their faces and necks, causing their hair to fall out (hence the need for wigs) and leading to serious gastric trouble and even death. Men used cosmetics as well as women. Eyelashes were blackened with old lamp-black, necessitating many remedies for sore eyes.

Even the unbrushed hairstyles led to trouble, causing one aristocratic lady to have a miscarriage on discovering mice in her hair. It was not unknown for the exaggerated hairstyles to catch fire if the owner sat too near a candle flame.

Home medication was drastic. Writing in 1779, Parson Woodforde describes how he cured his servant of a fit of ague by giving him a drink of gin, then pushing him into a pond, after which he ordered him to bed. He cured his own earache by sleeping with a roasted onion in his ear.

Teeth were bad and false teeth were made for the toothless wealthy, the plates being of wood, bone or ivory. By the end of the century the Wedgwood factory was supplying the paste for making china teeth.

By the end of the century also standards of personal hygiene were improving, largely because in this great age of fashion it was becoming fashionable to be clean. Beau Brummell, the trendsetter of the day, paid great attention to cleanliness, so the 19th century dawned to slightly sweeter smells for womankind.

The
Cottage

She had to fetch all her water from a spring a quarter of a mile from her cottage . . . in a very dry summer she had to go two or three miles

Only on Sunday would the cottage have presented such a tranquil scene; caring for her family in cramped conditions left little time for rest and relaxation during the week.
SUNDAY EVENING: Thomas Webster, (*Private Collection, Photo: Christopher Wood*)

The owners of stately homes in the 18th century liked to build mock rustic cottages in the grounds of their estates, to add a picturesque touch to their gardens, just as they added grottoes, Greek temples, newly-built castle ruins and even hermitages complete with live hermits. Their own lives were so secure that they evidently felt a need to evoke feelings of surprise, fear and melancholy in those who walked their garden paths.

They could have experienced all these emotions without difficulty if they had troubled to take a look inside many of the real cottages that existed at the time. These homes were not inhabited because they were picturesque or quaint, but because they had been the only homes known to the workers of the countryside for centuries.

Of necessity these cottages were built from local materials. Where there was stone, as in the Cotswolds, the north and in parts of Cornwall, they were built of stone. The little Welsh moorland cottage, Llainfadyn (123), was built in 1762 from heavy glacial boulders, and as slate was available it was used for the roof. It has a slate slab near the doorway as a draught excluder and a slate platform to keep some of the furniture clear of the earth floor. Many cottages eventually had their roofing changed from thatch to slate where this was available, because of the danger of fire. Where there were several homes in a village with thatched roofs it was usual to keep dragging hooks at the church to remove burning thatch.

Where there was plenty of wood cottages were timber-framed. The earliest of the timber-framed houses still in existence, known as cruck houses, date back to the 13th century. They were constructed with naturally bent timbers which formed an arch at each end of the cottage, and which can be clearly seen in the end walls today. The space between the arches was called a bay, and most of the early buildings consisted of a one-bay room, with a beaten earth floor, a fire in the middle of the room

and a thatched roof. The home could be extended as the family grew by the addition of another bay or more, to form a longer house, with a centre door and through passage to the back, the bay on one side of the passage often housing the family livestock.

The timber frames were filled with 'wattle and daub' walls which were woven wattle hurdles covered with a mixture of clay, dung and chopped straw. Some were plastered and painted, as in East Anglia; some were eventually tile hung, particularly in Kent, to give added protection against the weather; and in eastern counties some were weatherboarded for the same reason and painted white. Others had their timber frames brick-filled. In the south and west of England cottages were built of cob, a mixture of mud and straw that has lasted for centuries. A 13th-century cottage with flint walls has been reconstructed at the Weald and Downland Museum at Singleton in Sussex.

A woman often had to wait many years to get married until a cottage was available, usually when someone died. Or else she had to be content to wait until her proposed husband's friends helped him to build one, which was often done over night, whereby he could claim possession of a piece of land.

Cramped circumstances
In the Elizabethan period, when more living space was required, the cottagers usually made do by adding a lean-to extension at the back or side, with perhaps an added brick or stone floor and bread oven at one end. Chimneys can also be seen added on to the end of a cottage, enabling an upper floor to be built, lit by dormer windows cut into the roof. Many families simply slept in a small loft made by putting a few boards across one end of the roof. A rope or wooden ladder was probably all that was available to reach the upper floor until the 17th century, when some stairs at the side of the fireplace would be built. These were often cased in during the 18th

century to become a staircase, forming a much needed cupboard underneath the stairs.

This cupboard often contained a bed, and had doors that could be closed in the daytime. Box beds with wooden backs, sides and top could form a partition making an extra room and giving privacy to parents or to the girls of the family. These could have shelves at the back for extra storage. Inside the Welsh cottage in the photograph (123) boards rested on the tops of the two cupboard beds that divided the tiny cottage into two rooms, thus forming a loft reached by a ladder. Storage of the few possessions of the cottager was always a problem and cupboards were

built into any spare space and items hung on hooks from any convenient beam.

Where there was any room for it in a cottage the first acquisition of any value was the bed, and many homes that had little furniture of any worth downstairs had a four-poster bed upstairs, with curtains all round it: very necessary in a freezing bedroom with no fireplace. A hot brick wrapped in cloth was an early means of warming the bed, and a warming pan that could be filled with hot embers an early acquisition. Many warming pans had patterns or incised inscriptions of a biblical nature round the edges, now worn away with years of careful polishing.

The bed probably needed to be put

123 18th century cottage, Llainfadyn (*Welsh Folk Museum*)

125 Carrying water: after a
black and white drawing by
Gunning King (*page 126*)
(*Museum of English Rural Life*)

together in the bedroom because of the difficulty of getting furniture up the tiny staircases. For this reason chests of drawers and other larger pieces of furniture, when they did eventually appear in cottages, are found downstairs. Often some of the floorboards in a bedroom were left loose, so that large items that would not go up the stairs could be passed through the opening. Sometimes large items had to come down from the floor above, giving the opening the name of a 'coffin shoot' in some districts.

Beds, often found in every room of a cottage, had rush mattresses, and if the occupants were lucky, feather mattresses over these. Sometimes they had 'dust beds' or mattresses filled with chaff from the threshing, or flock mattresses filled with sheep's wool. These latter became lumpy very quickly and the wool had to be taken out, teased and put back into the cover.

In the 19th century many of the beds were half-tester beds, with posts and rails for curtains at the head end, giving protection from draughts for the head and shoulders only. In small homes the bed and chest were often the only items in a bedroom. Dressing and undressing often had to take place downstairs because the rooms were so small. A small truckle bed on wheels for a child could be pushed under a four poster bed in the daytime to make more room.

Cooking was at first done over a central

fire in a cauldron suspended from an upper beam. After the chimney was added to the cottage the cooking was done on the floor of the fireplace, in the down-hearth, where there would be a chimney crane on which to hang the pots. Trivets were used to stand small pots around the fire and bread was baked on an iron slab under a bake-iron. The slab was heated first in the fire, then swept clean with a home-made brush of twigs, and the food to be baked was put on it and covered with the bake-iron.

Baking once a week
At least as far back as Elizabethan times in the west country and Wales, a cloam oven (124) was used for baking, either standing free on the hearth or built into a wall. If was made of fireclay and was heated in the same way as the brick bread ovens with burning furze, turves or peat, or blackthorn wood which was a favourite fuel. When it was white hot the ashes were raked out and the bread or other food was put inside to cook. The clay door was closed, often being sealed with a little damp clay round the edges, which broke away easily when the door was opened. It took about an hour for the oven to heat up and an hour for the bread to cook. It was used mostly for a large baking once a week.

Many cottages had various sizes of the new-fashioned kitchen ranges installed when these became available, according to the space in the fireplace. In Cornwall the ironwork of the little ranges is particularly elaborately decorated and the knobs on the doors, the front bar and the supports for the small airing rack are of brass, all kept bright and shining with a weekly polish.

Where a cottage had a flat-topped range the housewife was at last able to cook in flat-bottomed saucepans, usually of iron, whereas when cooking was done for the most part on the down-hearth the saucepan with three legs, the skillet, which had been in use since Roman times, was the usual pan to balance on the ashes in the fire. In the same way the three-legged stool

124 Cloam oven, 16th–18th century

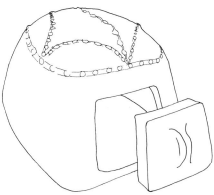

was the best seat for balancing on an uneven floor and the earliest type of Windsor chair so popular in country homes was a three-legged variety.

Carrying every drop of water needed in the home was a burden which we would regard as particularly arduous. In the absence of a well nearby, a village pump or a stream, the journey to get water, apart from what could be collected in a rain-water butt near the cottage, might be some distance.

A writer in 1875 describes meeting a poor woman in Surrey walking inside a hoop with a pail of water in each hand (125). The water was splashing all over her patched and worn-out gown. She told him she had to fetch all her water from a spring a quarter of a mile distant from her cottage. In a very dry summer she had to go two or three miles for water. She had three children, a pig and a husband who was a drunkard. Her children got a good slice of bread and sometimes a bit of treacle for their dinner, she said.

In spite of the hard life there seem to have been many healthy villages where the local doctor only attended at the beginning and end of life, and usually the local midwife dealt with the beginning without any help. Doctors were more plentiful at the end of the 19th century but had to be paid and would only have been called in when the illness could not be dealt with by home remedies.

Child care

Perhaps those housewives who could afford it bought a small vapour lamp sold in 1888 in which a germ-destroying liquid was vapourized 'for whooping cough, spasmodic croup, asthma, catarrh, colds, bronchitis, coughs, hay fever, sore throat, broncopneumonia, the bronchial complications of scarlet fever and measles and as an aid in the treatment of diphtheria', especially as it also dealt with 'the respiratory diseases of animals, as distemper and pneumonia in horses and dogs; gapes and roup in fowls'.

In many villages the parson's wife had taken the place of the lady of the manor in dispensing medicines to the villagers, but there were still numerous superstitions, especially concerning the treatment of children. At the end of the 19th century in Oxfordshire, a child ill with whooping cough was still passed through a naturally shaped bow of bramble, nine times on each of nine successive mornings. In Suffolk, babies were kept in the dark much of the time, in case the light should affect their eyes. The babies were not weighed, as it was thought this would prevent their thriving, and in any case a baby would not thrive well until it was christened.

By the end of the 19th century life in small cottage homes was becoming increasingly difficult. The days of self-sufficiency were over for them. In earlier centuries they had grown all their own food and kept a few animals, with perhaps a cow on the common land of the village. Gradually through the 18th and 19th centuries more and more of this land was enclosed and became private property, leaving the cottager with his small plot, perhaps the means to keep a pig and a few poultry, but little else.

The family pig was a most important member of the household and the killing of it provided one of the few feasts of the year, apart from Christmas and harvest time when an employer might give his workers a good meal. Every scrap of the pig was used and when salted down it provided the only meat available, with vegetable stew and perhaps a few dumplings, the main diet of country people.

Many people did not even keep a pig and meat was in very short supply for them. Their main meal time and time again consisted of potatoes and onions chopped up with a potato knife or 'teddy chopper' (127.1), and cooked in a little dripping in a frying pan over the fire. Small pieces of meat or slices of bread could be toasted in a down-hearth toaster (127.2). Potatoes were also baked in the ashes and raked out with a potato raker (127.3).

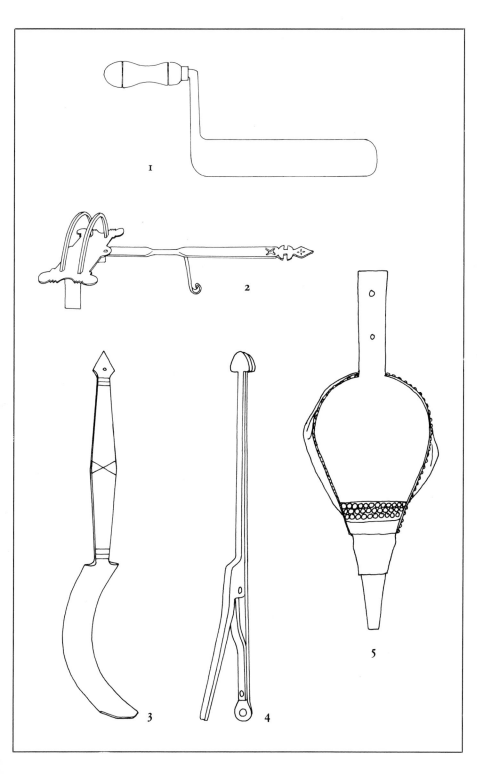

127.1 Potato chopper, or teddy chopper, 19th century (*Tiverton Museum*)

127.2 Bread or meat was placed between the hoops of this toaster (19th century)

127.3 Potato raker (19th century)

127.4 Brand tongs (19th century) (*page 128*)

127.5 Bellows (19th century) (*page 128*)

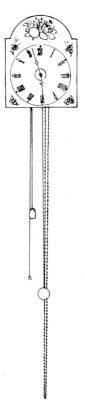

128 Dutch clock
(19th century)

brand-irons or tongs (127.4) for lifting glowing pieces of wood from the fire to light a rushlight, candle or pipe.

Lighting and heating

Iron candle snuffers (129.1) for trimming the wicks of candles were in use before the grander brass or silver ones, the wicks dropping when cut into the small container. The wicks of early candles did not burn away as do modern plaited wicks and needed constant trimming. A pair of scissors resembling small shears would also be kept handy during mending in the evening (129.2)

Oil lamps were used in homes that could afford them in the 19th century. The crusie lamp (129.3) had been in use in Scotland for long before that and was reminiscent of the lamps used in ancient Rome, full of oil with a floating wick made from a rush. In the late 17th century a lower section was added to catch the oil dripping from the overhanging wick above. The highlanders of Scotland burned fir-candles: splinters of resinous firwood from the pine forests, which could be held in a rushlight holder. Candles and rushlights made in the home were in use until the present century.

The stack of peat or logs outside the cottage, with bundles of furze tied into faggots, was not easily obtained. Many families suffered when wood became more difficult to come by. Coal was brought round to the villages on carts in large wicker baskets, but it was too expensive for the poorer families. They took their dinners to the village baker to be cooked in his large ovens for a penny or two, marking their pies with their initials for identification when they were collected. Bread was bought at the village baker rather than home baked. Increasingly the shortage of fuel forced the cottage women to do less baking and buy their food.

In Wales, Scotland and many northern counties of England oats had always been grown in larger quantities than elsewhere and a chest or kist of oatmeal was the housewife's wealth. On a griddle over the

In many districts the fire was of peat and was banked up at night with ashes laid over the peat turves, being brought to life again in the morning with some energetic blows from the bellows (127.5) that hung at the side of the fireplace. The fireplace was the centre of the cottage home with a Windsor chair and settle making the one warm corner for a family that spent so much time outdoors.

There might have been a long-case clock ticking away in the background, but from the middle of the 19th century a mass-produced American clock in a polished wood case was found in almost every farmhouse and cottage that could afford it. A cheaper clock was the Dutch one, which had a white-painted face ornamented with gay bunches of flowers (128). Around the fireplace hung the ladles and toasting forks constantly needed for cooking. There too might hang a pair of fire (130, 131.2) she cooked thin oatcakes which were spread with butter and eaten instead of bread, and a thicker variety which were dried on a home-made rack in front of the fire (131.1) and stored until needed. These were crushed with an oatcake roller (131.3) and eaten with butter-milk as a cereal. There are many recipes for making oatcakes, but a usual one was to mix four tablespoons of oatmeal with three tablespoons of water, a pinch of salt and half a tablespoon of melted bacon fat.

In Scotland, the oatmeal was made into porridge as well as oatcakes and served in staved wooden vessels, much the same as those from which the Elizabethans drank, but which often had hollow bottoms in which a few dried peas could be put, so that the bowl could be shaken to let it be known that a second helping was required.

Until the Enclosure Acts most cottage owners were poor but self-supporting. They could feed themselves in simple fashion from their own products, warm themselves and clothe themselves from their own homespun yarn. The men worked on their own holdings, even if they also worked as farm labourers on another man's land (for which at the end of the century they received about ten or twelve shillings a week), or as carpenters or blacksmiths for the village.

The most surprising thing is the number of occupations that were carried on in some of the small cottages, usually by the wives who needed to earn a little extra money to buy those articles that their homes could not supply, either from the local market or fair or from a travelling pedlar. Sewing materials, ribbons, spices, sugar, tea: – the list grew longer as the years advanced towards the 20th century and fewer items were made and produced at home. The factories in the towns began selling their products in country districts, gradually making money a necessity.

In certain districts women and children from poor homes worked on the land, weeding, or picking up stones that went to

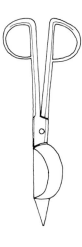

129.1 Iron candle snuffers (19th century)

129.2 Scissors used for trimming wicks (19th century)

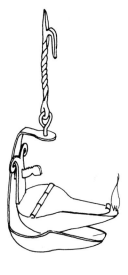

129.3 Scottish crusie lamp (19th century)

130 Oatcakes baking on a
griddle, drying on the fender
round the fire (*page 129*)
(*National Museum of Antiquities,
Scotland*)

make roads. They were busiest at harvest time but poorly paid for their hard work. When the last sheaves of corn had been lifted from the fields they went gleaning with their children to pick up every last grain of corn for themselves, which was eventually ground into flour for their baking. When the mother had to work in the fields, small children were often locked up alone in the cottage all day until their tired mother returned, and often terrible accidents occurred as a result.

Those women who could earn small amounts for work done in their own homes probably had better-kept cottages and better-looked-after children. In some districts, such as Dorset, they made buttons in the 18th and 19th centuries. Wire was brought by wagon from Birmingham, cut into different lengths and made into rings by the children. Then their mothers, working in various types of thread, covered the rings with buttonhole stitching, filling the centres with a variety of designs such as the 'Dorset cross wheel', 'honeycomb' and 'basket-weave'. These finished buttons were collected by agents in the surrounding villages and by 1840 these buttons were sold in Europe, Boston, Quebec and New York as well as all over the British Isles.

End of many cottage industries

The occupation ended in the same way as so many others with the advent of the Industrial Revolution. A button-making machine was shown at the Great Exhibition in 1851 and by the end of the 19th century the cottage industry had almost disappeared. The loss of a family's earnings in this way, small as it was, brought poverty and starvation to many homes.

In many small cottages there were few articles of furniture – just a board on a frame for a table, a few forms or stools, a bed, a chest – because much of the space was taken up with a weaver's loom (132). This was the case in many of the weaving villages of East Anglia. In cloth-making districts such as Berkshire the cottage

131.1 A special rack, for drying the oatcakes (*page 129*) (*Welsh Folk Museum*)

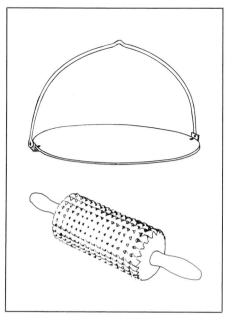

131.2 Griddle (19th century (*page 129*)

131.3 Oatcake roller or crusher, Welsh (19th century) (*page 129*)

132 Interior of a weaver's house in Skye, showing the weaver at his loom; Thomas Pennant, *A Tour in Scotland*, 1769 (*National Museum of Antiquities, Scotland*)

women with their spinning wheels were visited every week by agents from the clothiers of Reading and Newbury. They arrived with their pack horses laden with wool for the women to spin and every week they left with their packs laden with yarn ready for the loom. This village industry was again killed when machinery took the place of the spinners and weavers in their homes.

There were villages known for their glove making and some for their straw plaiting, used in the making of straw hats. Again the bundles of straw were brought to the cottages by cart for the women to split and plait into the various grades needed. Cottage women made cords for corsets and shoe laces and cane seats for chairs. One of the largest groups of home workers were the lacemakers in the areas around Honiton in Devon, Buckinghamshire, Oxfordshire, Bedfordshire and Northamptonshire. Here they made pillow-lace on a pattern of pins in their pillows, moving the threads with great dexterity with a collection of colourful bobbins, which were often elaborately decorated; many were given as love tokens.

Children taught to make lace

Pillow-lace had been introduced into England by Flemish refugees in the second half of the 16th century. The pillows on which the lace was constructed were made of hessian stuffed with straw and covered with a pillow cloth to keep the lace clean. Many humble lacemakers could not afford to buy the brass pins used and were forced to use fishbones. The lace they made was known as fishbone lace. Many lacemakers were taught as children in lace schools, held in a small cottage room crammed with children. The occupation did nothing for their posture or their eyes, and all lace-workers were glad if they could work outside in the summer months in better light.

Even when grown up several lacemakers often worked together in one cottage to save light and fuel. They worked with a lacemakers' candlestand (133.1), where one candle burned in a candlestick with glass bulbs fitted round it. When the bulbs were filled with water they reflected the light from the one candle on to the work of several workers seated round it. A single glass bowl was often put in front of a candle in the home to reflect the light and make sewing in the evening a little easier.

A lace-making machine was first introduced in 1760 and by the 19th century lace-making factories started the decline of the cottage industry.

The garment that was the mark of the countryman for many years was the smock, originally hand-made at home. From the Middle Ages until the 18th century the term 'smock' had been used for

133.1 Lacemaker's candle stand (19th century) (*Museum of English Rural Life*)

133.2 Apple scoops or corers (*page 135*) (*Welsh Folk Museum*)

134 Knitting in the Orkneys,
early 20th century
(*National Museum of Antiquities,
Scotland*)

a woman's undergarment, but it was then replaced by the term 'shift'. The heavy embroidery over the shoulders gave the man's smock thickness where it was most needed for outdoor work. Eventually smocks were produced commercially and sold at markets and fairs, though some were still made by village women for their own families or as outworkers for the factory. A woman could make about two a week and in 1850 received about two shillings and twopence per garment. The more elaborate smocks were kept for Sundays and special occasions.

While the women sewed many men carved, and with the aid of a small pocket knife produced ornate work such as the love spoons of Wales and apple corers or scoops (133.2) which were highly valued.

We think of cottage industries that involved sewing or knitting (134) as the usual occupations for women, but in the midlands, particularly round Bromsgrove in the Black Country, women and children produced hand-made nails and chains. This continued until less than a generation ago, when these cottage industries were organized into small factories, the women still doing the same work, but no longer in their homes.

Slowly more and more workers drifted into factories in the towns. With cottage industries no longer needed, the women had the alternatives of working in factories or staying at home in poverty. Their daughters were sent to domestic work in the homes of the local gentry or of the rising middle classes in the towns, often leaving home at the age of twelve, when their departure must have been a relief to the mother with one less mouth to feed. When they returned, as they often did, to marry a local boy, they missed the increased standard of living they had grown used to while in service, and did their best to introduce some of it into their cottage homes. They started to fill them with poorer copies of the factory-made furniture, the pictures and the ornaments that were eventually to overflow into the Victorian living rooms. The town had come to the country.

The Victorian Home

It never entered a Victorian housewife's head to consider whether or not a new article should be purchased because it might involve more work. There would always be someone to do it

'My Lady's Chamber': Walter Crane
(*Photo: Angelo Hornak*)

All through the 19th century men and women from the cottage homes of the country-side drifted in increasing numbers towards the towns. The growing prosperity of the middle class in industrial areas enabled them to build large family houses and these countrywomen in particular provided the many servants necessary to run them. They were poorly paid but there was no shortage of them.

The most usual type of town house they worked in was not easily run. It had anything up to four or five storeys, with basements for the servants to work in and attics in which they slept. The space for housebuilding in towns was at a premium and tall thin houses built in thousands were the result.

Outside the towns successful businessmen built miniature mansions set in large gardens. These homes were big by modern standards, but were smaller versions of much larger country estates.

The industrial workers in the towns, however, lived in the newly built rows of small back-to-back houses, so soon to become slums, with no cupboards, sinks, larders or water supply, and with one tap and privy for a whole row. The life of the lower classes in these homes was unknown to most of the more affluent members of society, and many of them did not learn how the other half lived until Charles Dickens described it so vividly in his novels.

In her spare time the mistress of the middle-class house was also able to read the novels of some of the great women novelists of the age including Jane Austen, George Eliot, Mrs Gaskell and the Brontes, most of whom kept their writing as secret as possible from their families and friends, sometimes writing under assumed names and often posing as men in order to get their work published.

Especially popular were the novels of Sir Walter Scott and those with a romantic and medieval flavour, which created a great interest in medieval architecture and highly carved furniture. Many homes and other buildings were given a Gothic flavour with turrets, battlements, Gothic-shaped windows, Gothic bookcases and stained glass in such unlikely places as bathroom doors.

Apart from books, there was an enormous increase in the number and variety of items that could be bought for the home by those who could afford them. These were mass-produced in factories whose owners were only too anxious to supply the needs of the fast-growing population, for there was no shortage of cheap labour or raw materials. It never entered a Victorian housewife's head to consider whether or not a new article should be purchased because it might involve more work. There would always be someone to do it.

Crowded and gloomy rooms

The heavy and ornate furniture now in the home, although of mahogany instead of oak, was reminiscent of similar furniture of the Elizabethan period, when there had also been increased prosperity among the middle classes. Chenille and embroidery covered everything in sight, including the mantelshelf, and even the legs of the tables and the piano that was now in many homes were covered. The whole room was ornamented with plants, photographs and knick-knacks of every description on 'what-nots'. These latter were stands, three or four feet in height, with several shelves and often with barley-sugar turned legs.

Added to the conglomeration of articles in a sitting room, making it seem more overcrowded and oppressive still, were the heavy plush curtains which hung over both doors and the lace curtained windows. The wallpaper, now the usual finish for walls, was heavily patterned in dark hues with the woodwork also in dark paint. Much of this dismal decoration was the practical answer to the smoke, soot and dust from coal fires, the high ceilings being built for the same reason. Spring cleaning only became an institution, indeed an

absolute necessity, in Victorian times.

Anything further removed than the Victorian home from the space, light and grace achieved by the end of the previous century is hard to imagine. The garden was a mass of evergreen trees and shrubs which did nothing to lighten the effect outside the house. With the Great Exhibition held in the Crystal Palace in 1851 the technique of glass set in frames of cast iron had been popularized and conservatories were built on to houses in increasing numbers.

Sunlight was not thought beneficial for either the furnishings or the occupants of

139 Heavy furnishings, potted plants, a blind to screen out the sunlight; *Summer*, by J. A. Grimshaw (*Courtesy of Christie's*)

the room (139). The large aspidistra in the window, with its leaves that were polished each day, was a plant that thrived in the dark and airless rooms, but it further decreased the light from the windows. Only at the end of the century and at the beginning of the 20th century did rooms have lighter decoration in walls and paintwork. Two-storey homes without basement or attic were then being built.

The Victorian bedrooms were just as congested as the living rooms but a little lighter in effect, with iron and brass bedsteads taking the place of the curtained four-poster from the middle of the century. The dressing table that was now common was often hung with white muslin.

Nineteenth-century married women were financially dependent on their husbands and socially inferior to them. Lawyers had always classed infants, lunatics, felons and married women together when they were considering persons of limited contractual liability. Until 1882 a married woman was incapable personally of holding or acquiring property and could not enter into contracts. Only the Married Women's Property Act of 1882 made the first changes in this situation.

For most wives it was back to the needlework and embroidery, with most of their days spent in their homes. They covered their homes with examples of their work, including antimacassars to keep the macassar oil used by their husbands on their hair from soiling the well-upholstered furniture.

The Queen set the example of complete domesticity, with a large family, and for the most part the women of the time followed her example. In any case, divorce was almost impossible, and women who did not marry were usually regarded with scorn. It was almost the 20th century before women could enter public school and university and so take up medicine, nursing, teaching or journalism. Only the more exceptional women from the end of the 18th century onwards were able to rise

above the difficulties and prejudice surrounding them.

Slowly they began to protest in writing, in such publications as *An appeal to the men of Great Britain on behalf of Women*, or *The female advocate or an attempt to recover the rights of women from male usurpation*. In 1825 William Thompson set out fully for the first time the argument for the full emancipation of women with a book entitled *Appeal of one half of the human race, women, against the pretensions of the other half, men, to retain them in political, and then in civil and domestic, slavery; in reply to a Mr. Mill's celebrated 'Article on Government'*. It was to be the 20th century before much of what he advocated was put into practice.

Victorian women's magazines

The more usual type of publication was the kind produced by Mrs Beeton's husband, Sam, in 1859: *The Englishwoman's Domestic Magazine*. It included articles on bringing up children and flower arrangement, and also articles on dressmaking. which offered readers the first paper patterns. Later they could get busy with their new sewing machines, when the first domestic Singer sewing machines were introduced in 1858.

Mrs Beeton wrote monthly supplements for the magazine which led in 1861 to her famous book on household management, written mainly for women in towns who were no longer expected to grow their own food or make their own medicines. It was taken for granted that everyone had the money to buy these things. The first instant foods such as Bird's Custard Powder appeared in 1840, and reliable tinned foods in the second half of the century.

In 1877 Jesse Boot took over the little shop in Nottingham where for years his mother had sold her herbal remedies, pills and potions. To these he added household goods and proprietary medicines, such as Allen's Hair Restorer, Woodhouse's Rheumatic Elixir, Beecham's Pills, Bragg's Charcoal Biscuit, Clarke's Blood

Mixture, Fenning's Cooling Powders and Woodward's Gripe Water. He bought in quantities large enough to sell them at prices within the reach of a large public and 'Boot's Cash Chemists' was born.

The railways, which were established by 1830, did take women out and about with a little more ease, even if only for the family seaside holidays that became so popular by the end of the century. But for the most part the home was their whole world. Entertainment consisted of musical evenings when the piano, with its pink silk panels, provided the background music to the entertainment, in which all were expected to take part. Sundays were devoted to strictly religious occupations,

as in Puritan times. There were to be no books read, except religious books, no toys or games allowed for the children and no sewing or embroidery for the women.

The households grew larger, there was a marked increase in the amount of clothing worn, particularly underclothes and more and more curtains and furnishings were hung everywhere, so laundering became a frequent and almost monumental task. For some time the idea persisted in smaller homes that only the poor had a weekly washday, and women strove hard to have 'a dozen of everything', particularly of underwear, so that frequent washdays were not seen to be an absolute necessity. In these homes a separate wash-

141 Mrs Lewis at the sink at Laundry Cottage, Sussex (*page 142*) (*Museum of English Rural Life*)

142 Iron stand
at Laundry
Cottage, Sussex
(*Museum of English
Rural Life*)

house was built to cope with the heat and steam, and a brick-built copper with a fire below to heat water and boil clothes became more common. This wash-house became a useful warm place to take a bath when the copper was alight to heat the bath water, the tin bath standing nearby.

Large country houses had separate laundry rooms unless the main wash was sent out to a local laundry or to someone in the village who ran a small laundry from her cottage. The photograph (141) shows a Mrs Lewis who ran such a cottage laundry in Sussex, which only ceased operating in 1953. She worked at a wooden sink fed only with cold water

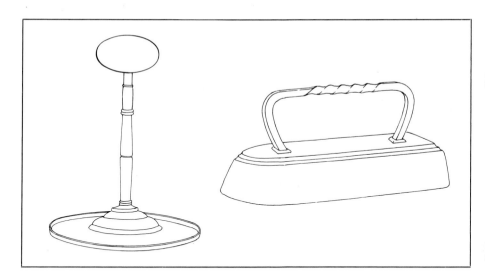

piped from a spring. The copper was filled by a hosepipe. She eventually acquired a stove for heating nine irons at a time, of a type usually found in larger laundries (142). It was an ordinary combustion stove with a central chimney. Racks for drying clothes were placed above these stoves. Where coppers were large enough to deal with great quantities of washing, the laundresses had to be provided with box-like stands to reach them.

Ironing was meticulously done and took several days. There were standing irons with differently shaped tops (143.1) which could be heated to cope with ironing those parts of garments which an ordinary flat-iron cound not deal with effectively. The fabric was passed over the top of these irons instead of the iron over the fabric.

There was a small iron with a curved bottom to press the inside of sleeves or to use as a polishing iron to give a glazed finish to starched linen or chintz covers. The convex bottom prevented the formation of lines. Heavy Victorian suiting was pressed with a large heavy iron known as a tailor's goose iron (143.2).

Labour-saving devices

To cope with the washing in large households a monster contraption known as a box mangle appeared, measuring about 1.80 metres long, 1.20 metres wide and 1.50 metres high (6 feet by 4 feet by 5 feet): an early 'labour-saving device'. It consisted of a large wooden box filled with stones or water. This stood on wooden rollers which ran on a flat bed of wood or slate.

The mangle in the photograph (144) was used on a large estate in Northumberland and was loaded with 12 large dressed stones, each weighing 50 kilogrammes (one hundredweight). The central wheel enabled the box to be wound to and fro with damp linen wrapped around the rollers. It was, reputedly, surprisingly easy to operate and it was said that in the hands of a skilled laundress a standard could be achieved high enough to make further ironing unnecessary. These mangles were still in use in the first half of the 20th century.

In some larger laundries, where water was available, the mangles might be connected to belting, worked by a water wheel. At Erddig in North Wales there was a drying cupboard, with drying racks which ran in and out on wheels, warmed from a small stove. In a cottage the housewife could only boil her washing in

144 Working a box
mangle (*page 143*)
(*Museum of English
Rural Life*)

the cauldron over the fire and on wet days dry it indoors anywhere she could. The chimney crane swung away from the fire was a useful spot on which to hang small items.

The first mechanical washer was a woman, working the clothes about in a washing tub with a wooden 'dolly', the end of which was like a wooden stool

(145.1). A more elaborate type with a conical copper end (145.2) was used for the same purpose, and there was a further version with a rubber end. In the second half of the 19th century a servant could work a rocking watertight box, containing clothes, water and soap, or a machine in which the movement was a rotary one, worked by a handle rather like a butter

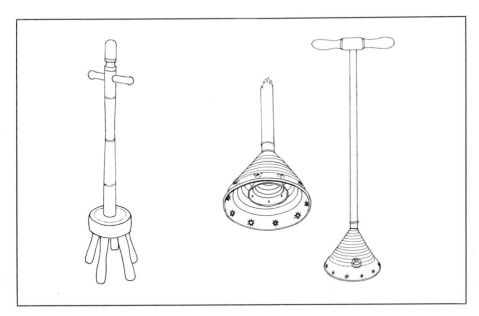

churn. Only about 1880 was the cast-iron clothes mangle introduced with large wooden rollers, turned by a handle, between which the laundry was pressed. A combined mangle and washing machine appeared at the same time, both of course hand-operated.

Gas for lighting was introduced into town homes after 1840 and by 1866 gas cookers were serious competitors to the solid fuel range. At the beginning of the 20th century there were gas rings, gas heated coppers and gas cookers, but electricity made no impression on kitchen power or appliances until after the First World War, although most large towns had electric power by 1860. Country homes missed out on gas and had to wait until recent years for electricity, even for lighting.

The leap forward in providing labour-saving aids in the home came when middle and upper class housewives found themselves with fewer servants when the war was over. Many domestic servants had no desire to return to their former employment after years of doing war work outside the home. More work in factories was available and it was to this that they turned.

Gas cookers at the beginning of the century were of cast iron, heavy, and difficult to clean. Gas coppers achieved popularity more quickly, for heating water was a constant chore. Carrying water was still a never-ending chore, and although it was now more usual for the kitchen sink to be supplied with running water in towns, there were no hot water systems in most houses before 1914.

The first plumbed-in bath

Baths when installed in wealthier homes were still usually filled by hand, though fully plumbed hot baths first appeared in the 1880s. They were large and of painted cast iron with a mahogany surround. The side of the bath in the bathroom at Lanhydrock House in Cornwall was so high a stool was needed to help the bather to climb in. This bathroom was installed at the end of the century for Lady Robartes, but her husband preferred to use a saucer-shaped bath in front of the fireplace in his own bedroom until his death in 1930.

By 1910 houses were being built con-

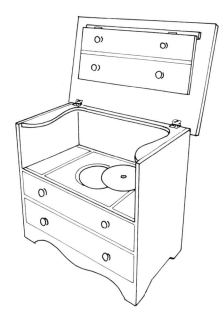

146.1 Bedroom commode disguised as chest of drawers (*North Cornwall Museum*)

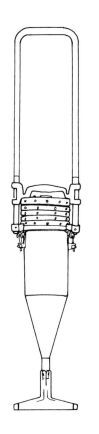

146.2 The 'Success Vacuum Cleaner', early 20th century (*North Cornwall Museum*)

taining bathrooms, some with porcelain baths. Gas geysers heated the water for some of them, but these were considered somewhat dangerous and probably at that time rightly so. Early showers were installed operated by a chain and by 1914 a variety of bathroom fittings appeared on the market, bath seats and soap trays, mirrors, bathroom scales, towel rails and toothbrush holders. Contemporary manufacturers were not slow in reacting to new fashions in the home.

Not until the end of the 19th century did toilet facilities improve. Water closets were installed in the home, but they were not shown off as obvious home improvements, being tucked away in the basement or in the yard at the back of the house. Commodes were the most usual toilet arrangement in a bedroom, usually heavily disguised, as is the one in the drawing (146.1), which when not in use masqueraded as a chest of drawers.

The usual washing facilities in the bedroom were a marble-topped washstand and with basin, jug and soap dish in a matching china set, and a can of hot water carried upstairs by the maid in the early morning.

Early morning chores

While one maid performed this service, another opened curtains and shutters, cleared ashes and laid and lighted fires. Friction matches were available for this purpose from 1826 onwards. After the kitchen fire had had its flues cleaned and had been lit, the first fire to be dealt with was in the breakfast room, which then had to be cleaned along with the hall and staircase. As well as the usual type of bellows to help get the fire alight a mechanical bellows was in use with a system of wheels inside, turned by a handle.

Apart from brushes and mops a rotary carpet sweeper might have been provided for the maid's assistance, and at the beginning of the 20th century came vacuum cleaners with bellows, some types of which required two women to handle them (147). With the 'Success Vacuum Cleaner' (146.2) the dust was collected by rubbing the end nozzle over the carpet and drawing it up when the handle of the pump was pulled up. In another type the upright handle had to be worked backwards and forwards to pump up the dust through a tube fitted into a hole in the central box.

These aids were needed more than in previous centuries as carpets were now common. The staircase was likely to have cast-iron rails with a mahogany handrail and a stair carpet. Cast iron was exploited everywhere in the Victorian age and was used for chair and table legs, bedsteads and garden furniture. It added to the already heavy look of the home. The table set for breakfast was probably the circular table with a central piller support that had appeared at the end of the previous century.

The maids were up and working by 5.30 and the family was not very far behind. Before breakfast was served at eight o'clock the daughters of the house would either have done an hour's piano practice or worked at their studies, and the mistress of the house, dressed in a morning wrapper, would have dealt with any urgent domestic affairs and visited the children in the nursery. Nursemaids were as readily obtainable as other servants and a family of any position kept the children in their own nursery world, visiting or being visited by their parents at set times of the day.

When a baby was born the mother was kept in bed for anything up to a month, and even a mother of fairly modest means could have a resident midwife for a month until she regained her strength. As she was more likely than not to be in the same condition the next year she probably needed this time to recover. Queen Victoria did mothers a great service when she gratefully accepted the use of chloroform at the birth of her eighth child, and after that it was widely used at childbirth for the relief of those who could afford it.

147 A bellows-type vacuum cleaner, the 'Wizard', in use around 1911 (*Crown copyright, Science Museum, London*)

Servants and family attended morning prayers and a reading from the family bible before breakfast. The servants usually ate breakfast at the same time as the family, and were not expected to wait on the family, who helped themselves. The food was kept hot on brass trivets in front of the fire, and included rolls and a dish of muffins. These could keep warm on a stand known as a 'cat' (148.1), because it sat by the fire and when put down always landed on its feet. The brass kettle boiled on the hob on the grate and the mistress of the house made the tea from an elaborate tea caddy, which was lined with lead foil and which had separate compartments for 'green' or 'black' tea, with room for a cut-glass sugar bowl between them.

The mistress often prefered to wash up

148.1 'Cat' or muffin
stand (19th century)
(*page 147*)

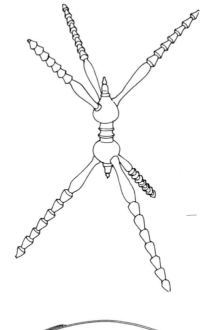

148.2 Knife tray
(19th century)

kitchen quarters. Colza oil, which came from rape seed, was used instead of the earlier whale oil, which had been very unpleasant to handle, but the lamps burning colza oil gave a rather dull light. Paraffin became popular for lamps about 1865 and replaced other oils. Candles were still widely used and a candlestick for each bedroom had to be cleaned and placed in readiness at the foot of the stairs.

Floor polish was home-made from candle ends, beeswax and turpentine, and furniture and floors were polished constantly. Paraffin was also used to clean windows and mirrors, the latter often of great size over mantelpieces.

The kitchen range

In large households roasting was still done on spits, but there was now one alcove, where formerly there had been an open fireplace, that was occupied by a closed-top kitchen range, on the lines of today's solid fuel cookers, made of cast iron which had to be blackleaded every day. Kitchen ranges were in common use by 1860, even in small kitchens. There was a fire in the middle of the range, an oven on one side and a hot water boiler on the other, but this boiler still had to be filled by hand. All the fire grates in the house had to be blackleaded until they shone, and living room fire-irons, pokers, tongs, shovels and fenders were of brass, all needing constant polishing. A point worth noting is that when all cooking was done on coal or wood fires the excessive heat of the kitchen continued all through the summer months as well as in winter.

Apart from cleaners and carpet sweepers, other labour saving devices were introduced to speed up some of the daily chores, such as knife trays (148.2) and cleaners (149.1) for cleaning several steel knives at once, and cast-iron mincing machines. There were intricate machines to perform simple tasks, such as an apple corer, turned by a handle, rather like a sewing machine. A cast-iron pressure cooker (149.2) speeded the cooking of food

her precious china herself after breakfast, putting it safely away in the special china cupboard in the breakfast room. This was probably a corner cupboard in daily use, not used merely for display purposes. There was no shortage of jobs to keep all the staff busily occupied all morning: bedrooms to be cleaned, beds to be made with their large feather mattresses, bolsters and pillows, dirty water from basins as well as chamberpots and commodes to be emptied and everything to be carried up and down stairs a thousand times.

Oil lamps, which were now in general use for lighting homes, had to be filled, cleaned and trimmed every day. Their cotton fibre wicks were boiled monthly in vinegar. Many houses had about twenty lamps to be attended to, and at Erddig a separate lamp room was set aside in the

149.1 Knife cleaner
(*Museum of English Rural Life*)

149.2 Pressure cooker
(19th century)
(*Museum of English Rural Life*)

in a pot. But it seems that as some jobs were made a little easier, others such as cleaning grates and cookers, looking after the increasing furniture and furnishings, and laundering more and more clothes, became more time-consuming.

Most domestic work needed a strong right arm, as even when labour-saving devices were introduced they were at first usually worked by turning a handle. In the kitchen (150), floors and table tops were scoured with sand, although polished linoleum and oilcloth were used as floor coverings in some kitchens, bathrooms and halls by the end of the 19th century. The stone floor of the scullery at Lanhydrock was cleaned with sawdust.

In 1881 the original 17th-century house at Lanhydrock was gutted by a fire which started, as fires so often have, in the kitchen chimney. When the house was rebuilt iron girders were used instead of timber, and it was further fireproofed by floors of concrete and ceilings of a patent fireproof composition. The inadequate water supply at the time of the fire had run out very quickly. It was clear that a better supply was needed and water for the new house was brought from Lanivet, three

miles away. A hot-water system and a central heating system were supplied by a boiler house below ground, a revolutionary move at the time. The house was also lit by electricity.

This modest home needed a large staff of servants with a large number of rooms forming the servants' quarters, including separate sitting rooms and bedrooms for both the butler and housekeeper. Then there was the servants' hall, stillroom, wine and beer cellars, gun room, kitchen, scullery, bakehouse, game and meat larders, cold room and dairy. The pantry and strong room were in the butler's quarters. The strong room contained the silver safe guarded by the pantry boy who slept there each night.

In most 19th-century houses of any size in town and country it was usual for the servants to work in the basement and to sleep in the attics. At least the Lanhydrock servants' quarters and kitchens were on the ground floor. There were separate staircases to the menservants' bedrooms and to those of the female servants. In those houses where candles were the only light, and there were many of these, the housekeeper dispensed 'servants' candles', small

150 The kitchen at Erddig, North Wales (*The National Trust*)

candles that burned for only half an hour, for the servants to take to their rooms. In the attic rooms at Erddig there was a sitting room where the maids spent their spare time and where they could do their own sewing.

The servants at Erddig were clearly well thought of and highly appreciated by their masters and mistresses, perhaps more so than was usual in the 18th and 19th centuries, although we cannot be sure of this. Certainly there is a unique collection of portraits of these servants, commissioned by their master Philip Yorke

between 1791 and 1796.

In the early years of the present century the practice of recording the servants was continued in this way, their master adding verses about their history. These tell stories of lives which must be similar to those of many such servants of the age, and show how the house and estate became almost their whole world. There is a photograph of Harriet Rogers, daughter of the estate carpenter who lived until he was 95 and was followed as carpenter by his son. Harriet entered service in 1853. Her sister was a children's nurse and she herself first became a nursemaid, followed by twelve years as a lady's maid. She was photographed in 1911 when she was cook-housekeeper at Erddig, having spent her life in the various occupations of millions of unknown women throughout history.

There are photographs of groups of servants in 1912 and 1852, when the female staff are the laundry maid, dairy maid, head housemaid, lady's maid, head nurse, and cook-housekeeper. These were obviously only the senior female staff. In 1912 the group included the head nurse, head and second laundry maids, housemaid and under-housemaid, cook and housekeeper (152).

The large kitchen at Lanhydrock was within a reasonable distance of the dining room and there was a serving room next to the dining room which had a hot-cupboard, heated by hot water pipes, where the food could be kept hot after it was passed through a hatchway from the kitchen quarters.

Lady Robartes' sitting room where she dealt with household matters was next to the servants' quarters. The steward of the estate had his room in this part of the house, and the smoking room and billiard room were here also, well away from the family living rooms. Smoking was not approved of by Victorian ladies and required special clothes for the men and a special room where they could indulge in the habit.

Churns full of milk were delivered from the farms on the estate to the dairy scullery, where dairy maids made large quantities of butter and prepared Cornish cream on a special scalding-range heated by hot water pipes. The main dairy was used principally for the storage of the dairy products and had a marble slab in the middle, with a cold-water cooling system, on which were kept jellies, blancmanges and the elaborate cold puddings so popular at the time. Soups, custards, junkets and milk puddings for the nursery were also kept fresh here. In the 1870s the first ice refrigerators were introduced. They were made of wood and lined with zinc.

There were separate larders for meat, fish and dry groceries. In the fish larder was a shallow copper box where a whole salmon could be kept warm over hot water while it was being carved. Jams, jellies and chutneys were the housekeeper's province and prepared and kept by her in the still room, which had its own kitchen, the housekeeper taking over the role of the medieval lady of the manor.

For so large a household (and at Lanhydrock the servants' quarters are larger than the family's), there was a bakehouse with a large bread oven which provided all the bread, scones, cakes and biscuits required. The oven had a proving oven below where the kneaded dough was put to rise. The oven and all the fires at Lanhydrock used coal by the truckload. The large amounts of coal used in towns led to the thick fogs of which Charles Dickens left such vivid descriptions in his novels. At Erddig the bakehouse ovens were heated with wood and faggots in the same way as a cottage bread oven, but both these larger ovens whether using wood or coal took several hours to heat up to bread-baking temperatures.

For Lady Robartes in her sitting room, supervising the staff, arranging meals with the cook and dealing with all the domestic details of her large household, the day must have been fully occupied. But in the 19th century every household, except the poorest, could have one or more servants. The mistress of the smaller home then found herself with little to do. For millions of Victorian women the promise of the 18th century for leading a fuller life outside their homes never materialized. Ironically, at a time when they were given so much help in the home, the taboos of the times prevented them from taking advantage of this freedom. Their frustration was to increase as the 20th century got under way, but year by year their slow progress towards female emancipation continued.

The world was to change in ways which the Victorian housewife could never have

visualized in her wildest dreams. She could never have guessed that her daughter, so secure and contented at the beginning of the century, would live through two devastating world wars, each of which were to push women out of the home into the outside world as never before; that she would see inventions and developments that would revolutionize both marriage and domestic life, ranging from the automatic washing machine to the Pill; that transport would speed up on land, sea and in the air, taking mankind, with womankind not far behind, from the pennyfarthing to the moon rocket; that there would be crashes both financial and moral resounding in her ears with depressing regularity and that the whole of life from all corners of the world would be brought right into her home, by radio and later by television.

That same daughter has survived all this and has become one of the many indomitable 80-year-olds we have around us today, who for the life of them can't understand when their daughters are always so tired or even why they are occasionally tired themselves. It gives one hope for the future, a quality which for the housewife, whatever or wherever has been her place, has never been in short supply.

Castles, Houses and Cottages to Visit

The following are some of the many homes open to the public in England, Scotland and Wales which illustrate the points raised in this book:

Athelhampton, Dorset
Avebury Manor, near Marlborough, Wiltshire
Bayleaf Farmhouse, *see* 'Weald and Downland' in Museums section
Berkeley Castle, near Bristol, Gloucestershire
Bodiam Castle, near Hawkhurst, East Sussex (The National Trust)
Brading Roman Villa, Isle of Wight
Breamore House, near Fordingbridge, Hampshire
Caister Castle, Great Yarmouth, Norfolk
Carisbrooke Castle, Newport, Isle of Wight
Cawdor Castle, Nairn Highland, Scotland
Charlotte Square, No 7, Edinburgh (The National Trust of Scotland)
Chastleton House, Moreton-in-Marsh, Gloucestershire
Chedworth Roman Villa, Gloucestershire (The National Trust)
Chirk Castle, near Wrexham, Clwyd
Clandon Park, near Guildford, Surrey (The National Trust)
Compton Wynyates, Tysoe, Warwickshire
Corfe Castle, Dorset
Cotehele House, Calstock, Cornwall (The National Trust)
Culzean Castle, Maybole, Strathclyde, Scotland (The National Trust of Scotland)
East Lambrook Manor, South Petherton, Somerset
Edinburgh Castle, Scotland
Erddig, near Wrexham, Clwyd (The National Trust)
Eyhorne Manor, Hollingbourne, Kent
Fishbourne Roman Palace, Chichester, Sussex
Gaulden Manor, Tolland, near Taunton, Somerset
Great Chalfield Manor, Melksham, Wiltshire (The National Trust)
Great Dixter, Northiam, East Sussex
Ham House, Petersham, Richmond (The National Trust)
Harvington Hall, Kidderminster, Hereford and Worcester
Jane Austen's Home, Chawton, Hampshire
Kennixton Farmhouse, *see* 'Welsh Folk Museum' in Museums section
Killerton, near Exeter, Devon (The National Trust)
Lanhydrock House, near Bodmin, Cornwall (The National Trust)
Leeds Castle, near Maidstone, Kent
Littlecote, near Hungerford, Berkshire
Little Moreton Hall, Congleton, Cheshire (The National Trust)
Lullingstone Roman Villa, Kent
Manorbier Castle, near Pembroke, Dyfed
Mary Arden's House, Wilmcote, Stratford-upon-Avon, Warwickshire
Mompesson House, Salisbury, Wiltshire (The National Trust)
Norman House remains, Christchurch, Dorset
Old House, The, High Town, Hereford and Worcester
Old Post Office, The, Tintagel, Cornwall (The National Trust)
Osterley Park House, Isleworth (The National Trust)
Paycocke's, Coggershall, Essex (The National Trust)
Pendean Farmhouse, Sussex, *see* 'Weald and Downland' in Museums section
Powis Castle, Powys (The National Trust)

Rockbourne Roman Villa, near Fordingbridge, Hampshire
Royal Crescent, No 1, Bath, Avon
St Fagan's Castle, Cardiff
St Nicholas Priory, The Mint, Fore Street, Exeter, Devon
Saltram House, Plymouth, Devon (The National Trust)
Scaplen's Court, High St, Poole, Dorset
Souter Johnnie's Cottage, Kirkoswald, Strathclyde (The National Trust for Scotland)
Stourhead, Stourton, near Mere, Wiltshire (The National Trust)
Tattershall Castle, Lincolnshire (The National Trust)
Townend, Troutbeck, Cumbria (The National Trust)
Trerice, St Newlyn, East Cornwall (The National Trust)
Uppark, Petersfield, Hampshire (The National Trust)
Washington Old Hall, Tyne and Wear. (The National Trust)
Weaver's Cottage, Kilbarchan, Strathclyde (The National Trust for Scotland)
Wilton House, Hampshire

Prices of admission and times of opening can be found in *Historic Houses, Castles and Gardens* published by ABC Historic Publications and in *Stately Homes, Museums, Castles and Gardens of Great Britain* (Automobile Association). Admission to National Trust properties is free to members of the Trust.

Museums

Some of the articles for domestic use mentioned in the book can be seen at the following museums; many have rooms furnished in period style.

Abbot Hall Museum of Lakeland Life and Industry, Kendal, Cumbria
Abbey House Museum, Kirkstall, Leeds, West Yorkshire
Angus Folk Museum, Kirkwynd cottages, Glamis, Tayside
Anne of Cleves House, High St, Lewes, East Sussex
Arlington Mill Museum, Bibury, near Cirencester, Gloucestershire
Aston Hall, Trinity Road, Aston, Birmingham
Avoncroft Museum of Buildings, Bromsgrove, Hereford and Worcester
British Museum, London
Castle, The, Colchester, Essex
Castle Museum, York
Corinium Museum, Cirencester, Gloucestershire
Cornish Country Life Museum, Summercourt, near Newquay, Cornwall
Christchurch Mansion, Ipswich, Suffolk
Dorset County Museum, Dorchester, Dorset
Elizabethan House, Fore Street, Totnes, Devon
Geffrye Museum, Kingsland Road, London E2
Highland Folk Museum, Kingussie, Inverness
Moyse's Hall Museum, Bury St Edmunds, Suffolk
Museum of East Anglian Life, Stowmarket, Suffolk
Museum of English Rural Life, Whiteknights Park, Reading, Berkshire
Museum of London, London Wall, EC2
National Museum of Antiquities of Scotland, Edinburgh
North Cornwall Museum and Gallery, Camelford, Cornwall
Oak House Museum, West Bromwich, West Midlands
Ordsall Hall Museum, Salford, Greater Manchester
Oxfordshire County Museum, Woodstock, Oxfordshire
Pennine Farm Museum, Ripponden, West Yorkshire
Reading Museum and Art Gallery, Reading, Berkshire
Red House Museum, Christchurch, Hampshire
Rowley's House Museum, Shrewsbury, Salop
Ryedale Folk Museum, Hutton-le-hole, North Yorkshire
Salford Museum and Art Gallery, Greater Manchester
Stranger's Hall, Charing Cross, Norwich, Norfolk
Tiverton Museum, Tiverton, Devon
Tudor House Museum, Southampton
Weald and Downland Open Air Museum, Singleton, Sussex
Welsh Folk Museum, St Fagans, Cardiff, South Glamorgan
West Yorkshire Folk Museum, Shibden Hall, Halifax, West Yorkshire
Winchester City Museum, Winchester, Hampshire

Opening times can be checked in *Museums & Galleries* published by ABC Historic Publications and in *Stately Homes, Museums, Castles and Gardens of Great Britain* (Automobile Association).

Further Reading

BARING-GOULD, S *An Old English Home* (Methuen) 1898.
BENNETT, H. S. *The Pastons and their England* (Cambridge) 1970.
BOON, GEORGE C *Calleva Atrebatum at Silchester, Hampshire.* (Reading Museum) 1972.
BRADFIELD, NANCY *Historical Costumes of England* (Harrap) 1970.
BRAUN, HUGH *Old English Houses* (Faber) 1962.
BRYANT, ARTHUR *The Medieval Foundation* (Collins) 1966.
    – *Protestant Island* (Collins) 1967.
BURRARD, SIDNEY *The Annals of Walhampton* 1874.
BURTON, ELIZABETH *The Georgians at Home* (Longmans) 1967.
    – *The Elizabethans at Home* (Longmans) 1970.
    – *The Early Tudors at Home* (Allen Lane) 1976.
CAMPBELL, MILDRED *The English Yeoman under Elizabeth and Early Stuarts* (Merlin Press) 1960.
COULTON, G. G. *Life on the English Manor* (Cambridge) 1937.
COX, J. STEVENS *Dorset Dishes of the 17th century* (1967) and *Dorset Folk Remedies* (1970) The Dorset Natural History and Archaeological Society.
DITCHFIELD, P. H. *The Charm of the English Village* (Batsford) 1908.
DODD, A. H. *Life in Elizabethan England* (Batsford) 1961.
EMMISON, F. G. *Elizabethan Life* (Essex Record Office) 1976.
FLETCHER, RONALD. *The Parkers at Saltram* (B.B.C.) 1970.
FLOWER, BARBARA and ELIZABETH ROSENBAUM. *The Roman Cookery Book* (Harrap) 1958.
FRASER, ANTONIA. *Mary Queen of Scots* (Weidenfeld and Nicolson) 1969.
FUSSELL, G. E. and K. R. *The English Countrywoman* (Melrose) 1953.
GRANT, I. F. *Highland Folk Ways* (Routledge and Kegan Paul) 1961.
Guide to the Antiquities of Roman Britain (British Museum) 1964.
HARRISON, MOLLY. *The Kitchen in History* (Osprey) 1972.
HARTLEY, DOROTHY *Food in England* (Macdonald) 1962.
    – *Life and Work of the People of England.* 6 volumes. (Batsford) 1931.
HAYDEN, ARTHUR *Chats on Cottage and Farmhouse Furniture* (Unwin) 1912.
HOLE, CHRISTINA *The English Housewife in the 17th century* (Chatto and Windus) 1953.
HOSKINS, W. G. *History from the Farm* (Faber) 1970.
    – *The Midland Peasant* (Macmillan) 1957.
JEKYLL, GERTRUDE *Old English Household Life* (Batsford) 1975.
    – *Old West Surrey* (Longmans, Green & Co.) 1904.
Jewellery through 7000 years (British Museum) 1976.
JOBSON, ALLAN *Suffolk Yesterdays* (Heath Cranton) 1944.
JOHNSTON, DAVID *Roman Villas* (Shire Archaeologies) 1979.
KEOGH, BRIAN and MELVYN GILL *British Domestic Design Through the Ages* (Arthur Barker) 1970.
LABARGE, MARGARET WADE *A Baronial Household of the 13th century* (Eyre & Spottiswoode) 1965.
Lady's Magazine 1801.
LASLETT, PETER *The World We have Lost* (Methuen) 1965.
LIVERSIDGE, JOAN *Britain in the Roman Empire* (Routledge and Kegan Paul) 1968.
MACFARLANE, ALAN *The Family Life of Ralph Josselin* (Cambridge) 1970.
MORLEY, HEWITT A. T. *Roman Villa, Rockbourne, Hampshire.* Report 1969.
PARKER, ROWLAND *The Common Stream* (Paladin) 1976.
PLINY *The Letters of the Younger Pliny* (Penguin) 1963.
SCOTT, AMORET and CHRISTOPHER *Collecting Bygones* (Max Parrish) 1964.
STENTON, DORIS MARY *English Society in the Early Middle Ages* (Penguin) 1965.
    – *The English Woman in History* (Allen and Unwin) 1957.
STENTON, SIR FRANK *Anglo-Saxon England* (Oxford) 1943.
THOMPSON, FLORA *Lark Rise to Candleford* (Penguin) 1973.
WARNER, PHILIP *The Medieval Castle* (Weidenfeld and Nicolson) 1971.
WEST, TRUDY *The Timber-frame house in England* (David and Charles).
WHITELOCK, DOROTHY *The Beginnings of English Society* (Pelican) 1968.
WILSON, DAVID *The Anglo-Saxons* (Pelican) 1971.
WOODFORDE, REV. JAMES *The Diary of a Country Parson* (Oxford) 1968.
YARWOOD, DOREEN *The English Home* (Batsford) 1956.

Index